AF578009

AT DEATH'S DOOR

A TRUE STORY OF SURVIVAL
AGAINST IMPOSSIBLE ODDS

AT DEATH'S DOOR

50 DAYS BETWEEN LIFE AND DEATH - AND THE GOD WHO DIDN'T LEAVE

GREG HERSHBERG

www.rabbigreg.org
At Death's Door

Cover Designers: R. Roush and J. Martin

Editors: T. Jolee and R. Clark

This memoir is a truthful recollection of events in the author's life, presented as accurately as memory allows. Any inaccuracies or omissions in names, details, or places are unintentional and may be attributed to the strain and circumstances the author experienced during that time.

Aneko Press
www.anekopress.com
inquiries@anekopress.com

Aneko Press, Life Sentence Publishing, and our logos are trademarks of
Life Sentence Publishing, Inc.
203 E. Birch Street
P.O. Box 652
Abbotsford, WI 54405

BIOGRAPHY & AUTOBIOGRAPHY / Religious

Paperback ISBN: 979-8-88936-586-0
eBook ISBN: 979-8-88936-587-7

10 9 8 7 6 5 4 3 2 1

Available where books are sold

Contents

All praise to God, the Father of our Lord Jesus Christ. God is our merciful Father and the source of all comfort. He comforts us in all our troubles so that we can comfort others. When they are troubled, we will be able to give them the same comfort God has given us.

—2 Corinthians 1:3-4 (NLT)

To my wife, Bernadette,
and my children, Jeremy, Shaina, Max, and Lily,
who inspire me each day.
I am so thankful for the life we have together.
And to Jesus,
who carried us when I could not.
I love You with all my heart and soul.

INTRODUCTION

THE GOD OF ALL COMFORT

WHEN I SAT DOWN TO WRITE THIS BOOK, I DID NOT HAVE A POLISHED OUTLINE OR A STRATEGIC PLAN. What I had was a story, a testimony of what it is like when everything in your life changes overnight, and when it's hard to make sense of it all. It is a story that is still being written.

If I am honest, what I have endured over the last several years with my health is complicated. There are unresolved moments, unanswered questions, and prayers that have drawn me into deeper reflection before the Lord. As a rabbi raised in a God-fearing Jewish home, and someone who has spent my life teaching about Jesus, I have found myself wrestling through a season of affliction I never expected. I am still learning what it means to trust the Lord when life throws curveballs your way.

When I began putting words to these pages, I thought about people moving between hospitals, medical tests, and waiting rooms while carrying the grief that comes when the body begins to fail. I thought about the single parent who wakes each morning determined to keep going despite exhaustion and fear. I thought about those growing older and facing limitations they never anticipated, and the caregivers who faithfully carry burdens few people ever understand. I thought about prisoners who feel forgotten, believers living without religious freedom, grieving parents returning to empty homes that once overflowed with life, and professionals whose identity begins to unravel when careers end.

Most of all, I found myself thinking about Jesus.

I thought about the Messiah who stepped into human suffering, who wept with mourners, touched the sick, and spoke hope to those who society overlooked. Scripture describes Him as *a man of pains, well acquainted with illness* (Isaiah 53:3 CJB). Jesus understands suffering and grief in ways we often struggle to comprehend. This book is my testimony of what I walked through with Him. It tells the story of a chapter of my life I never planned to live through, and in many ways, it is still being written each day.

I have written several books over the years. Teaching and guiding others in their faith journey is a major part of my calling. But this book feels different. In many ways, it feels like a capstone. I originally intended to write these words for my family as something they could hold on to long after I am gone. Yet as I started to reflect on my medical crisis, I sensed the Lord inviting me into deeper vulnerability. This book became my attempt to share what it truly looks like to walk with God when we do not have all the answers. This kind of pain is no longer theoretical but deeply personal.

I do not share my story to glorify myself or to glorify suffering. Suffering alone holds no power to redeem. I write to glorify our Savior who meets us in the midst of suffering and reveals the Father of mercies and the God of all comfort. The comfort described in Scripture is not a shallow encouragement or a fleeting sense of relief. In ancient Hebrew understanding, emotions were not seen as originating from the mind or even the heart, as we often think today in Western culture. Instead, they were believed to arise from the inner organs – especially the womb or bowels. So when the Bible speaks of God having compassion, it is not referring to surface-level sympathy. His love and mercy are visceral, deeply internal, and profoundly parental. Colossians 3:12 (KJV) calls it the *bowels of mercies,* and the Gospels describe how Jesus was *moved with compassion* (Mark 1:41 NLT) toward the sick. This is the kind of comfort He gives.

The apostle Paul learned this through his own personal suffering. He endured persecution, affliction, and physical pain. Yet through those trials, he discovered a truth that continues to shape believers today. God's comfort is not given only to sustain us. It is given also so that we may then comfort others. Out of our deepest sorrows flows living water that can empower and strengthen our brothers and sisters. I would soon discover this reality in ways I never expected.

During my long hospital stays, I was living in a strange paradox. I was fighting for my life, yet somehow I was still serving. I gave away more than seventy-five copies of my book *Don't Die in Your Sins* while in the hospital. Doctors would stop by just to tell me they loved me. Nurses stayed past their shifts to talk or pray. I had never been physically weaker, yet I had never known the presence of God so deeply. Faith carried me when understanding could not. I could not see it then, but now I understand. *El Rachum,* "The Compassionate God," was restoring my heart and teaching me what it truly means to live surrendered. I had known about His love before, but in that season, I came face-to-face with His holiness.

If there is one thing I've learned, it's this: The Holy Spirit is still leading us, even when everything we built feels like it's falling apart. He walks with us through the valley. Sometimes

He changes the situation, sometimes He changes us; but He never leaves us. God doesn't expect fake strength. He gives us room to grieve, wrestle, and still believe.

So if life feels raw, uncertain, or messy right now – hear me clearly. God loves you. He is present. He is a compassionate Father and the God of all comfort, *especially* in the valley of affliction.

Now, let me tell you what happened on the day my life changed.

> *Even though I walk through the valley of the shadow*
> *of death, I will fear no evil, for you are with me;*
> *your rod and your staff, they comfort me.*
> —Psalm 23:4 (ESV)

– CHAPTER ONE –

EVERYTHING GOES BLACK

MOST OF THE TIME WHEN YOU WAKE UP IN THE MORNING, IT IS BUSINESS AS USUAL. What I mean by that is that you get up and go about your day. It feels ordinary and predictable. The sun rises, coffee brews, and you put on some pants. Most of us live that way.

November 13, 2023 began as any other day, but everything was about to change. I had no idea that day would change my life forever.

The whole weekend leading up to it felt like a gift. That September, my wife, Bernadette, surprised me with anniversary tickets to see Jerry Seinfeld and Jim Gaffigan live in St. Louis. Now, I currently live in the South, but I grew up in the Bronx. Jerry Seinfeld is my contemporary, a New York Jew like me, and I've always appreciated his clean comedy. Bernadette and I decided to turn the trip into a full weekend getaway. We flew to St. Louis on Friday feeling great and hopeful. The plan was simple – enjoy the city, see the show, and come home refreshed.

Friday was beautiful. We toured the city like a couple of teenagers. We visited the Gateway Arch, that massive steel monument overlooking the Mississippi River, a gateway into what was once unknown territory. We rode up inside it and looked out over the city and the river below. We took a boat ride along the Mississippi. We walked through the Missouri Botanical Gardens holding hands like newlyweds, instead of a couple moving closer to their golden years.

Bernadette and I genuinely enjoy each other's company. After decades of raising Jeremy, Shaina, Max, and Lily while building Beth Yeshua International from absolutely nothing, we were entering a season where life felt different. The kids were grown. The ministry was flourishing. Over the years, we had planted hundreds of congregations worldwide and reached tens of thousands of prisoners with the gospel. Each week, people from all over the globe tuned into our broadcasts, and we felt deeply grateful for the season we were in.

That Friday night over dinner, Bernadette and I talked about what our future might look like. In just two months, we had a Panama cruise planned to celebrate my sixty-fifth birthday. Beth Yeshua was approaching its twentieth anniversary. I had been thinking about stepping back from the daily grind of ministry – not retiring completely, but easing into a slower rhythm of life. I imagined spending more time in Florida, walking the beach, enjoying early dinners, and simply being present with my family.

Life was full in the best way possible.

Saturday, we spent another full day exploring the city. It had been a beautiful, relaxed day, the kind where everything feels easy and light. But by late afternoon, I began to notice something wasn't right. I didn't feel sick exactly, just . . . off, and I couldn't explain it.

When we went out to dinner that evening, the discomfort intensified. I couldn't shake the sense that something was wrong, even though I couldn't put my finger on it. By the time we got back, I lay down for a while and finally said to Bernadette, "I don't think I can go to the show tonight. I can't even move."

But that's not how I'm wired. I remember lying there thinking, *Come on, Greg. Get it together. Put on your big-boy pants and push through. You didn't come all this way to sit in a hotel room. Stop complaining and get moving.*

So that's exactly what I did.

We went to the show Saturday night. Seinfeld and Gaffigan were both hilarious, but I sat through it feeling miserable, doing my best not to let it show. I couldn't enjoy any of it. Afterward, we headed straight back to the hotel, and by the time we arrived, I was completely drained. I watched a little television, then went to bed early, hoping a full night of sleep would correct whatever was happening to me.

It didn't.

By Sunday, I was completely bedridden in the hotel room. It wasn't like having the flu or running a fever. It was worse because there was no pattern, no explanation, nothing I could measure or wait out. Exhaustion settled over me in a way I had never known before. There is a particular kind of alarm that sounds when the nervous system begins sending signals you cannot interpret, when you recognize something is radically wrong yet you cannot name it. Long before I was willing to admit it intellectually, an unmistakable awareness was already rising beneath the surface that my life had crossed into unfamiliar territory. I was no longer in control of where it was heading.

Monday morning, November 13, I woke up in that hotel room with a deep, unshakable sense that something wasn't right. I couldn't explain it at first. When I swung my legs out of bed and stood, a heaviness settled into my chest – not sharp pain, but a dense pressure that didn't belong, as if something inside me was pressing downward from within.

Bernadette was already up, zipping her suitcase and

organizing our things. She has always been the one who keeps us on schedule. She looked over at me, and her expression changed immediately.

"You okay?" she asked.

"Yeah," I said quietly. "Just tired."

But I wasn't just tired.

I felt awful. And I mean awful in a way I had never experienced before.

A LIFE DISRUPTED

We left the hotel very early in the morning, heading to Lambert International Airport. The sky was covered with thick gray clouds, one of those hushed Midwestern fall mornings where the air is cool but oppressive at the same time. I remember staring out the car window at the overcast St. Louis skyline, trying to convince myself I was fine. That I just needed to get home. That whatever this was would pass once I was back in Macon, Georgia, back in familiar territory.

But I knew better. Deep down, I knew something was profoundly wrong.

Now, let me give you some context. I'm six foot three, and I've tried to take care of my body throughout my adult life. Even into my sixties, I was riding my bike twenty-five miles at a time, getting to the gym several days a week, and swimming in open water. Staying active was a normal part of my life, and I was committed to my health.

Part of that came from losing my father when I was fifteen years old. He was only fifty-five, a strong man, an Army Ranger in World War II, a marksman who received the Bronze Star for bravery and a Purple Heart after being wounded by a grenade. When I watched two strangers carry his body out of our apartment, it left a mark on me that never faded. It planted a deep awareness of how fragile life really is, and how quickly even the strongest among us can fall.

I never wanted to go down that road. So I did everything I believed I was supposed to do. I exercised regularly. I ate well. I disciplined my body. I believed health was wealth. Take care of your body, and your body will take care of you.

But life does not operate like a formula. You can do everything right and still find yourself standing in front of something you never prepared for. When life begins to unravel, the plans and structures you once depended on can collapse without warning. James was right: Life really is but a mist, *a mist that appears for a little time and then vanishes* (James 4:14 ESV). And sometimes that realization doesn't arrive gently. Sometimes it comes all at once.

By the time we reached the airport, I was in bad shape. Not tired. Not run-down. It was something deeper than that. My body felt like it was turning against me, as if something fundamental inside had shifted.

Thankfully, we had plenty of time to check in. Bernadette stepped up to the counter to handle our TSA PreCheck, and I told her, "I don't feel right. I'm going to go sit down for a minute."

She looked at me carefully. Bernadette has always been able to read me better than anyone. I could see concern begin to flicker across her face.

"You want me to come with you?" she asked.

"No, no," I said. "Go ahead. I'll just sit over there."

I started walking toward a small seating area near the gates. The airport was buzzing with life, people rolling suitcases behind them, business travelers checking their phones, families trying to keep track of kids and carry-on bags. It was just another Monday morning. Everyone was moving normally.

Except for me.

Suddenly, the chairs looked farther away than they should

have been. Each step was like slogging through mud, my legs refusing to cooperate as the distance stretched in front of me. I kept moving, placing one foot in front of the other, reaching for something stable to hold on to.

And then something strange happened. The airport began to tilt. Or maybe I did. I can't tell you which came first. I just know that one moment I was reaching for a chair, trying to steady myself, and the next moment the floor was rushing up toward me. Then everything went black.

When I opened my eyes, I was lying flat on my back in the middle of the airport's main thoroughfare. Fluorescent lights hummed overhead, sharp and disorienting. A few people lingered nearby, watching from a distance as travelers continued moving past. Two figures leaned over me with calm urgency. "Sir? Can you hear me?"

My mouth was dry. My head felt stuffed with cotton, like my thoughts were moving through fog. I tried to make sense of where I was and how I had gotten there.

"What . . . what happened?" I asked.

"You collapsed," one of them said. His voice was steady, reassuring. He had kind eyes, the kind you hope to see when you're scared and don't understand what's going on. "Airport personnel called for help. We're EMTs. What's your name?"

"Greg. Greg Hershberg." I tried to sit up, instinctively, stubbornly. "I need to get to my gate."

"Sir, you need to lie down." His hand pressed gently but firmly against my shoulder. "We're going to take you to the hospital."

"No." The word came out sharper than I meant it to. "I'm fine. I just need to get home." But I wasn't fine. I knew it, even then. And they knew it too.

At the counter, Bernadette was still sorting things out when the agent glanced past her and said, "Ma'am, your husband is lying on the floor." Bernadette looked over and saw me stretched out a short distance away. Without missing a beat, she smiled and said, "Oh, he's fine! He'll sleep anywhere!"

And honestly, she had every reason to think that. Over the years, I had fallen asleep in airport chairs, waiting rooms, couches, and once even on a park bench when I was completely exhausted. That was just me. Bernadette knew it better than anyone.

Humor has always been our way of navigating tense moments, and she genuinely believed I was simply resting. One of the agents responded, "Ma'am, he's not sleeping. He collapsed in the middle of the walkway!" That's when Bernadette moved. My wife walked quickly toward me, the humor fading from her face as the seriousness of the moment settled in.

EMS explained that protocol required them to take me to the hospital – no exceptions. But I begged them to let me fly home instead. I told them about my doctors in Macon, friends who knew my medical history, people I trusted. I didn't want to end up in an unfamiliar hospital in a strange city. I can be persuasive when I need to be. Maybe they saw the desperation in my eyes. Maybe they saw Bern's face and realized there was more happening here than a simple medical incident. Perhaps it was God's mercy at work. For reasons I still don't fully understand, they agreed. They placed me in a wheelchair and rolled me toward the gate. By then, I felt terrible, foggy and weak, barely aware of what was happening around me.

The flight to Atlanta passed in a haze. I sat there drained, slumped in my seat, trying to hold myself together. When we landed, I needed wheelchair assistance just to get to our car. That alone should have alarmed me. I'm not someone who asks for help. I'm not someone who struggles to walk through an airport.

But there I was, being pushed through the terminal like a man I barely recognized.

We drove the hour and a half from Atlanta to Macon. When we got home, I collapsed onto the couch and stayed there for the rest of the day and into the night. I kept telling myself sleep would fix it, that I would wake up the next morning, and everything would return to normal. Whatever it was, it would pass.

It didn't.

The next morning, Tuesday, November 14, I was significantly worse. The pressure in my chest had deepened. The exhaustion was thickening and ominous. And the dull ache I had been trying to ignore was sharpening into something I could no longer dismiss. That was when I finally admitted I needed to go to the emergency room.

Now, let me tell you something about me. I don't go to the ER unless I'm bleeding out of my eyeballs. Over the last twenty years, I've had seven aneurysms repaired and have undergone multiple major surgeries. Hospitals and I have a history, and not a good history. I deal with PTSD connected to medical trauma. A friend once told me that post-traumatic stress disorder isn't limited to battlefields; that trauma can develop anytime the brain and body experience overwhelming fear, pain, or loss of control. At the time, I nodded politely, but I didn't fully understand what he meant until I began recognizing how hospitals affect me.

Psychologists explain that when someone experiences repeated crises, the brain doesn't simply store those memories as past events; it stores them as *warnings*. The brain is designed to protect us, so when it recognizes sights, sounds, or smells connected to prior trauma, it can trigger a response before the mind has time to reason through what's happening. People move into a hypervigilant state, and fight-or-flight mode kicks in. The heart rate increases. Breathing changes. Muscles tense. Senses sharpen. The body reacts as though danger is already present, even when you are technically safe. It's not weakness. *It's survival wiring.*

When I walk into a hospital, I don't just see rooms and equipment. I *feel* memories. I *feel* fear. I remember and relive all the times those stuffy, sterile rooms closed in on me with a sense of doom. Something inside me recoils, like every cell remembers the pain before I can even name it. I brace for impact, and the walls press in with the terrifying thought that I might never leave.

God's Word addresses this human reality in a way that has always stood out to me. Throughout the Bible, God repeatedly tells His people, *"Do not be afraid,"* or, *"Fear not."* Notice He does not say, "Do not *feel* afraid," because sometimes we are downright terrified. Feelings often rise before the mind has time to reason with them. God never denies the emotional reality of fear; He calls us to anchor ourselves in Him despite it. David captured this tension with remarkable honesty when he wrote, *When I am afraid, I put my trust in you* (Psalm 56:3 ESV).

We even see this reflected in the life of Jesus Himself. In the Garden of Gethsemane, as He faced the suffering that was about to unfold, the Gospel of Luke tells us that He prayed in deep anguish and that His sweat became like drops of blood falling to the ground (Luke 22:44). Many medical scholars have connected this description to a rare condition known as hematidrosis. Under extreme emotional or physical distress, the body's stress response can become so intense that tiny blood vessels surrounding the sweat glands rupture, causing blood to mix with perspiration. His body endured acute psychological trauma, and His fear was real. Jesus experienced the full weight of pressure, sorrow, and dread – yet He was without sin and continued to surrender Himself to the will of the Father.

That truth has always meant something to me, but it took on an entirely different weight when I found myself facing yet another hospital visit, another unknown diagnosis, another moment where I felt my life slipping away. So when I finally told Bernadette we needed to go to the ER, she didn't argue or hesitate.

She simply nodded.

Because she knew.

It was bad. Really bad.

> *"For sighing has become my daily food;*
> *my groans pour out like water.*
> *What I feared has come upon me;*
> *what I dreaded has happened to me.*
> *I have no peace, no quietness;*
> *I have no rest, but only turmoil."*
> —Job 3:24-26 (NIV)

– CHAPTER TWO –

ANY DAY BUT THANKSGIVING

TWO YEARS BEFORE MY MEDICAL CRISIS, I TAUGHT A SERIES AT BETH YESHUA CALLED "THE MYSTERY OF SUFFERING." Week after week, I opened the book of Job before our congregation and walked carefully through his story. At the time, I believed every word I taught, and I still do. But I understand now that there are truths you can know intellectually from Scripture, and then there are truths you come to know in a deep, personal way when your own life collapses.

By then, I understood suffering in more than one way. As a rabbi, I had seen it up close through the pain of others. I had sat with families in hospital rooms, stood beside them in funeral homes, and spent long nights in living rooms where the silence gripped the atmosphere. Over time, I had learned what sorrow looks like when it fills a room.

I also knew suffering personally. Long before November 2023, my own body had failed me more than once. I had already endured major surgeries, terrifying recoveries, and the kind of medical battles that leave a man alive – but changed. I also lost my father as a teenager. So when I taught on suffering, I was not teaching theory. I was teaching Scripture with scars. All of it was very real to my life.

In that series, I told my congregation something that I still believe is essential if we are going to speak honestly as believers. Job was a righteous man. He was not suffering because God was exposing some hidden scandal in his life. He was not being punished for secret sin. The text says he was blameless and upright, that he feared God and shunned evil. In other words, his suffering was *not* a consequence. It was a *mystery.* And that matters, because one of the cruelest things we do to people in pain is rush to explanations that make *us* feel safer instead of making *them* feel seen.

Job's friends sat in silence at first, which was wise. Then they opened their mouths and began to wound him with their theology. They could not wrap their minds around the fact that a righteous man could suffer so deeply, so they built a theory that blamed him.

I have watched believers do this for years, often with good intentions, and still do damage. When someone we love is hurting, there is a powerful temptation to say something – anything – that might make the moment feel less heavy. We reach for explanations, spiritual clichés, or quick answers because silence feels uncomfortable. But too often those words end up wounding rather than helping. My advice is simple: resist the urge to fix the moment with your words. One of the most spiritual things we can do is sit with someone in the ashes and be present without pretending to have all the answers.

During that sermon, I also taught that Job suffered in rapid succession, wave after wave of loss, and that his pain was incomprehensible. Sometimes, well-meaning people come to me and say, "Greg, I'm having a Job season," and I know what they are trying to say. They mean life has become heavy. They mean the losses are piling up. They mean they are hurting, and they cannot make sense of what God is allowing. I understand that, and I never want to be dismissive of anyone's pain. But Job's suffering was not just a "bad week" or a "hard stretch." Job lost ten children. He lost his livelihood. He lost his security. He lost his health. He was covered in agonizing sores and was scraping his skin with broken pottery just to get a little relief. His losses came so quickly and so violently that even his friends sat speechless when they first saw him. The Bible does not hide the reality of suffering. It tells us the truth about it.

Scripture gives us language for sorrow. It gives us lament, which is not the absence of faith but the expression of faith in pain. It gives us the book of Lamentations, where grief is spoken plainly before God, and sorrow is not cleaned up for public viewing. It gives us Joseph. It gives us David. It gives us Hagar in the wilderness, Hannah in her anguish, Naomi in her bitterness, and Mary and Martha grieving at their brother's tomb. It gives us Elijah under the broom tree, asking God to take his life. It gives us Paul saying he was so utterly burdened beyond his strength that he despaired of life itself. It gives us Jesus Himself and all He endured.

The Bible does not hide human anguish. It teaches us how to bring it all to God.

When I taught that series, I knew suffering is a normal part of the human experience. What I did not know was how soon I would be forced to learn those truths again in a deeper way. I was about to move from teaching the mystery of suffering to inhabiting it in real time.

WE NEED TO GO

Before I tell you about that Tuesday morning, I need to give you some medical background, because my hospital story did not begin in November 2023. By then, I had already been through more than my fair share. I was born with a connective tissue disorder, a genetic condition that affects the strength of the blood-vessel walls and makes me more prone to aneurysms. An aneurysm is a weakened area in a blood vessel that begins to bulge outward under pressure. In major arteries, especially the aorta and the iliac arteries, a rupture is life-threatening. Without immediate medical intervention, survival may be measured in minutes to a few hours.

In October 2005, when I was in my mid-forties and raising four young children, I came as close to death as a man can come and still be here to talk about it. Doctors discovered a massive aneurysm in my iliac artery measuring nearly twelve-by-eight centimeters, roughly the size of a grapefruit. The surgery to repair it was complicated, and the days that followed were even worse. A serious complication landed me in intensive care for more than two weeks, where I fought infections and learned to stand and walk again after my body had been pushed to its limits.

By the grace of God, I recovered. In the years that followed, I faced more surgeries, including multiple aneurysm repairs in 2019 and 2020. Stents and grafts were placed throughout my vascular system, and my life became a cycle of scans, follow-ups, and waiting for the next report. Along the way, I came to understand a particular kind of fatigue that follows a body with a long medical history.

But I kept going. I exercised. I rode my bike. I stayed active. I did what I had always done. I trusted God, kept moving, and refused to make a career out of feeling sorry for myself. In all, I have endured more than twenty years of physical suffering.

So when I finally told Bernadette that we needed to go to the emergency room on November 14, she knew it was the last place I wanted to be. I was not just bringing my current symptoms with me; I was dragging in decades of medical baggage that needed its own luggage cart.

The decision to head to the ER was not dramatic. That is one of the details I want to preserve, because crises in real life are often less theatrical than people expect. There was no one moment at home when we both shouted and ran for the car. What happened that Tuesday morning was calmer and, in some ways, more sobering than panic. I woke up and realized the stories I had been telling myself were no longer believable.

The weakness had not lifted. My body felt heavy in a way that was hard to explain. When I sat up, the dizziness was still there, and the strange internal sense that something was deeply wrong had not faded. I also had no appetite, which for me was a sign and wonder in itself. I really enjoy a good meal. Men like me can be very creative with our self-talk when we are trying to avoid the obvious. But that morning, those explanations no longer sounded convincing. This was not exhaustion. I was sick.

I simply said to Bernadette, "We need to go to the hospital." She looked at me, read my face the way only a wife of many years can, and said, "Okay. Let's go."

She drove, and I sat in the passenger seat watching an ordinary morning move along as if nothing in the world had changed. Traffic was steady. People were headed to work. Someone was carrying coffee into their office. Someone else was walking their tiny, well-manicured dog. It is amazing how cruelly normal the world can look when your own body is beginning to fail. And there is a loneliness in that, not because God is absent, but because your crisis is invisible to everyone except the person sitting beside you, and the Lord who sees all things.

I remember feeling not so much terror in that moment as disorientation. I still thought, or maybe *wanted* to think, that this was a detour. I thought we were going to get a diagnosis, get medication, get instructions, and go home. I was not yet living in life-and-death language in my own mind. I was still thinking in terms of inconvenience, interruption, and recovery.

When we got to Piedmont Hospital in Macon, there was an unexpected mercy waiting for me. A trusted doctor-friend of mine named Dr. Wilfredo Rios was working as the attending physician that day. If you have ever had a complex medical history, you know what a gift that is. It is no small thing to be seen by someone who already knows your baseline, your background, your temperament, and your history. With all I had been through, I did not present to the ER casually. My friend knew that. He knew I was not there because I was having a nervous spell or because I wanted reassurance. If I was there, something was genuinely wrong.

They began running tests, all the usual and necessary ones. Bloodwork, panels, cultures, all of it. While I waited, I found myself doing what most people do in that situation: I started negotiating with the best possible scenario. I thought maybe I had COVID or the flu. It seemed plausible. *Chest pressure. Deep exhaustion. Weakness.* I went through the checklist in my mind. I figured they would diagnose something manageable, give me a prescription, and we'd be on our way.

I was already mentally rearranging the next few weeks in my mind. Thanksgiving was nine days away. The kids were coming home, and I was so excited. We had family plans. Hanukkah was around the corner. We had that cruise scheduled for my birthday in January. I was lying there trying to make room for a temporary illness inside that life, not realizing that life itself had already changed categories.

Doctors ran several tests and eventually discovered community-acquired pneumonia in the lower lobe of my right lung. The diagnosis seemed reasonable enough. After all, I had just been on an airplane, and travel often brings home more than souvenirs. They sent me on my way with some basic medication, and for a moment, we felt relieved. It sounded like something that would pass with rest and a few days of treatment.

But things did not improve. In fact, they began to move in the opposite direction.

By November 16, my condition had deteriorated so much that I had to be rushed back to the emergency room. This time, we knew something was wrong, *very* wrong. The doctors ordered more tests, and soon the answers arrived.

When the physician finally entered the room, he did something that immediately caught my attention. He pulled up a chair and sat down. Doctors rarely sit when they have routine news. He told me I had a blood staph infection – *Staphylococcus aureus* – circulating in my bloodstream.

I heard the word *infection* and, for a brief moment, my mind translated it into something manageable. Infection meant antibiotics. Infection meant treatment. Infection meant this was miserable, but fixable. I was not immediately thinking of catastrophe. Then he kept talking. He explained that a bloodstream staph infection was not like a minor infection you treat and move past. It was serious, potentially life-threatening, and could lead to major complications. Then he said the number that changed the emotional temperature of the room in an instant: about twenty percent of people who develop this infection die from it.

One in five.

I want to tell you the truth about that moment, because it did not happen the way people think these moments happen. I did not burst into tears. I did not start panicking. I just sat there stunned. I thought, *Maybe I misunderstood you.* So I asked him, "I'm sorry, did you just say one in five?"

Because that's *twenty percent!* Twenty percent is a big number. I could easily be the one in five.

They started me on Vancomycin immediately, a very strong, broad-spectrum intravenous antibiotic used for serious bloodstream infections. The cultures would take time to come back, and in a situation like mine, they could not afford to wait. When bacteria are in the bloodstream, doctors have to act quickly, often before they know exactly which strain they are dealing with or what it is resistant to. Vancomycin is one of the heavy hitters in that situation.

In my case, it became another turning point. My kidneys did not tolerate it. The very medication meant to fight the infection pushed me into acute kidney failure. Soon, a nephrologist came in, and I started on dialysis. So now I was not only battling a life-threatening blood infection, but I was also facing renal failure. It was as if the treatment itself had become another problem to solve. By that point, I was pretty swollen and yellow. The story kept getting worse faster than I could emotionally metabolize it.

This is one of the things I wish more people understood about life-threatening situations. It is not only the pain itself that wears you down, but it is also the *succession.* It is the way one hard thing becomes another before you have finished absorbing the first. It is the way your future starts collapsing while you are still trying to process the present.

After a while, your spirit grows tired of bracing for impact. You begin to wonder if anyone in the room is ever going to say something hopeful. At one point, I even caught myself thinking, *Can somebody say something good? Or maybe just stop talking for a minute?*

There is something else I need to pause and say here, especially to the men who read this, and even more so to those who lead. As pastors, rabbis, fathers, and spiritual leaders, we are often trained, implicitly or explicitly, to be steady. We are the ones who pray for others. We carry the vision. We are the ones people look to when things fall apart. But there is a word we do not talk about enough in those circles: *despair.* After that first week in the hospital, I found myself closer to that word than I had ever been before. I had reached a place where I was mentally and emotionally drained in a way I had never experienced in my life. It was dark, and in the weeks to come, it would get darker. The fiery darts of the Enemy came fast and strong. I was exhausted from fighting, exhausted from processing, exhausted from trying to remain composed when my body had been so completely rocked.

And yet I was still fighting in my own way. I was doing push-ups each day in the hospital room. I still believed I might make it home for Thanksgiving.

I was not faithless.

I was depleted.

And there is a difference.

David describes this kind of exhaustion in the Psalms with striking honesty. In one place he writes, *I am weary with my crying out; my throat is parched. My eyes grow dim with waiting for my God* (Psalm 69:3 ESV). In another he pleads, *Be gracious to me, O Lord, for I am languishing; heal me, O Lord, for my bones are troubled* (Psalm 6:2 ESV). David was a king, a warrior, a man after God's own heart, and yet the Psalms show us that he was not afraid to bring his weakness before the Lord.

Job speaks with an even deeper rawness. His suffering stripped away every polite religious phrase until only the truth remained. At one point, he cries out, *"Why did I not perish at birth, and die as I came from the womb?"* (Job 3:11 NIV). Later, he confesses the torment of sleepless nights: *"The night drags on, and I toss till dawn"* (Job 7:4 NLT).

God is not offended by honest prayer. The God of Israel is not fragile. He invites truth. Sometimes the most faithful prayer a person can utter is simply, "Father, I have nothing left." That was the place I had reached. My pain and suffering were very real. Darkness had descended upon me.

As the days in Macon went on, more concern gathered around my case, and with good reason. Because of my connective tissue disorder and prior surgeries, I had grafts and stents in my vascular system. Blood staph infections are notorious for seeding themselves in synthetic material. This means the bacteria can attach themselves to those artificial pieces inside the body and settle there. When that happens, the infection becomes much harder to eliminate because antibiotics have a more difficult time reaching and fully clearing it. And in my situation, that possibility made everything more serious. It also raised another troubling question for the doctors: if the bacteria had attached themselves to one of those grafts or stents, they might have to remove it entirely in order to stop the infection.

I looked at the doctor and thought, *This is surreal.* I knew they were doing their job. They were not trying to frighten me. They were being responsible, transparent, and medically thorough. But lying there, hearing that conversation while already dealing with blood staph and kidney failure, it felt as if the horizon kept moving farther away.

Moments like that change the way you pray.

My words were not polished. They were not sermon-ready. I cannot tell you exactly what I said, but I know it was probably something simple, something like, "Lord, have mercy," or, "Father, help me!" When life hits you hard enough, faith gets stripped down to what is real. Sometimes the most sincere prayer you can offer is nothing more than a few tears.

By then, the CDC had come through my hospital room, specialists were in and out, and I was no longer telling myself this was a short hospital stay. The local team did everything they could, but I was not improving. The pain was increasing. The imaging was not giving clear answers. Another physician friend of mine, a man I trust deeply, came to see me and took one look at me and knew this had gone beyond what should be handled locally. He urged transfer to Emory University Hospital in Atlanta, where my vascular surgeon and his team had handled my previous aneurysm repairs.

Emory is one of those places you go when things are complicated, when the case requires a deeper bench, more specialization, and more experience with unusual vascular problems. It was the right move, but right does not always feel comforting when you are the one on the gurney.

The transfer was arranged for Thanksgiving Day.

I preferred any day but Thanksgiving.

By then, my children were home, and there is very little in this world I treasure more than sitting at the table with my wife and them. As I tried to rest, my mind kept drifting to what that day was supposed to look like. I could picture the table set with turkey and all the food, hearing the laughter overlapping as everyone talked at once, the way we always do. I love those moments. Instead, I was headed to another hospital.

The ride felt endless. Pain stretches time, and fear stretches it even more. My hands were trembling, and I remember just asking Father God for mercy. My mind kept moving from one face to another. I was thinking about my children. I was thinking about Bernadette. I was thinking about our congregants, people I love deeply, and I found myself asking God for more time, more strength, more years to serve them.

The whole way to Atlanta in that ambulance, I was praying. Hoping. No, I was *begging* God for a miracle.

STAY AT HIS FEET

When I finally arrived at Emory late that night, there was no room ready. That is not a complaint, just a fact. Hospitals are complicated places, and transfers require handoffs and timing and systems larger than any one patient. I lay on a gurney in a hallway for hours before they got me into a room around midnight.

Bernadette and the kids followed in the car and arrived

before I did because of the traffic. By then, we were all exhausted. My wife carried her own pain, though at the time I did not fully understand the depth of it all. Caregivers suffer in ways people rarely talk about. Spouses and children who walk hospital corridors day after day carry a weight that is different from the patient's, but no less real. There is even a name for it. Psychologists call it anticipatory grief – the sorrow that begins before the outcome is known.

When you sit beside a hospital bed and do not know whether you are preparing for recovery or goodbye, something in your heart begins grieving already. It's the ministry of the caregiver. It's sacred work that most people never volunteer for but simply find themselves entrusted with. It is the steady presence in the chair beside the bed. It is the quiet strength when fear is pressing in. It is the private conversations with doctors when the patient cannot yet bear the weight of what might be coming. Most of all, it's the tears they hold in because someone in the room needs them to be strong. My sweet Bernadette was all of that.

Even when I began writing this book, revisiting these memories was difficult for both of us. For me, they were events I endured in my own body. For her, they were moments she watched unfold with her own eyes. When she remembers them, they do not feel like distant history. The memories are still fresh and raw. Watching someone you love suffer is one of the toughest human experiences to describe. The pain leaves a mark that does not simply disappear when the crisis ends. I understand that more clearly now than I did then. A person does not get sick alone. An entire family walks through it together. Everyone is impacted.

That first night at Emory, once I was finally in a room and the movement around me slowed enough for my thoughts to catch up, I remember lying there and asking a question that kept returning in different forms: *What happened?* Not as an accusation, but as stunned bewilderment. *How did a weekend in St. Louis become this? How did an airport collapse turn into a bloodstream infection, renal failure, dialysis, transfer to Emory, and Thanksgiving in a hospital bed? How did life pivot this hard, this fast? Lord, how do I walk through this valley with courage even when I'm afraid?*

I did not have an answer that night. In fact, I would learn that one of the hardest disciplines in suffering is to stop demanding an immediate explanation in exchange for perseverance. Job did not get a neat answer. Paul did not get spared every affliction. Elijah still had to walk through his exhaustion. What they received, and what I would receive in ways I did not yet understand, was the presence of God in the middle of the storm.

The Bible says God keeps our tears and records them (Psalm 56:8). David wrote those words while hunted, displaced, and in deep distress. He was declaring that none of our grief is invisible to God. None of it evaporates into the air. Jesus sees. He remembers. He attends to it all.

In the ancient world, mourners sometimes kept what were called tear bottles. When someone died, or great sorrow struck a household, a person might collect their tears in a small vessel as a visible expression of grief and remembrance. Those tears were not meaningless. They were a testimony that love had been present and that loss had been felt. When David wrote that God keeps our tears, he was drawing on that imagery. The sorrow of God's people does not fall unnoticed to the ground. The Lord personally regards the suffering of His people. Our deepest sorrow is acknowledged by the King of Glory.

That night at Emory, I did not feel triumphant or extra holy. I felt weak, shocked, and painfully vulnerable. But I was not abandoned. And though I did not yet understand how deep the valley would go, I knew this much: My Shepherd was still with me. This was not the end of the crisis. It was only the threshold of a valley far deeper than I had ever walked in before.

What I learned in that season is something I want to pass on to you. The greatest miracle in your life is not when God changes your situation.

The greatest miracle is when suffering does not change your position.

Stay at His feet.

When it's silent – stay.

When it's dark – stay.

When you feel forgotten – stay.

Because one day you'll look back and realize:

Jesus was never distant.

He was always with you and drawing you deeper.

> *Deep calls to deep at the roar of your waterfalls; all your breakers and your waves have gone over me* (Psalm 42:7 ESV).

– CHAPTER THREE –

THE THIEF COMES IN THE NIGHT

THERE IS SOMETHING NOBODY TELLS YOU ABOUT BEING CRITICALLY ILL. The physical pain is real, and it is terrible. But the thing that truly grinds you down, the thing that reaches into the places medicine cannot touch, is what happens in your mind at three o'clock in the morning when the room is dark, and your heart is darker.

That is where the real war is fought. It's the Enemy's playground.

By the time I was settled into Emory, I had already been in the hospital for days. My body was under siege, battered by a staph infection in my bloodstream, and acute kidney failure brought on by the very medication that was meant to fight it. I was on dialysis. Tubes ran in and out of me. My body was stretched tight with fluid and pain. I have a fairly high pain tolerance, but this was beyond all of that. This pain was building every day into something I had never encountered before.

And the nights were something else entirely.

Hospitals do not actually sleep. That is one of the first things you learn. People think it gets quiet after midnight, but it does not. Nurses move in and out of the room at all hours, checking machines, adjusting tubes, whispering to one another in the half-light. Machines beep. A patient in another room begins to moan. Blood is drawn. And just when you finally start to drift off, just when your body begins to surrender for ten minutes of mercy, the cleaning crew shows up at four o'clock in the morning to change the trash-can liner. That is hospital sleep. It comes in scraps. In interruptions. After a few nights as a patient, lying helplessly at the mercy of the hospital staff, your mind enters a strange state of psychosis. At Emory, the nights did not pass; they pressed in.

Every time I closed my eyes, something would pull me back into the darkness. And during those long, excruciating, sleepless nights, I became very aware that something other than my medical team was working on me. Satan himself was on the hunt, and I was a prime target. I want to tell you about that, because I think it is one of the most important parts of this whole story.

As God's people, we cannot afford to be ignorant of Satan's schemes. He is a bully. If you study the Bible carefully, you begin to notice a pattern: the adversary does not usually attack when people are strong. He waits for moments of weakness, exhaustion, fear, or transition. From the beginning of time, the Enemy has targeted God's people when they are most vulnerable.

When the Lord delivered Israel from Egypt, their freedom had barely begun before they were under attack. In the wilderness, the Amalekites came against them and struck those who lagged behind – the weary, the weak, the children, the women, the sick, and the disabled at the rear of the camp (Deuteronomy 25:17-18). They did not confront the front lines where the warriors stood ready. Instead, they targeted the stragglers, the ones most vulnerable in the long march through the desert. It is an ancient pattern, and it reveals something about the nature of the Enemy. He does not usually charge where strength is gathered. He looks for the tired, the wounded, and the ones who have fallen a step behind.

We see the same pattern in the life of Jesus. After forty days of fasting in the wilderness, when His body was depleted, and His human strength had been stretched to its limit, the devil chose that time to rattle Him (Matthew 4:1-3). The tempter looks for those moments to break our spirits.

God's people are called to be alert, sober-minded, and grounded in truth. Peter gives us a vivid warning when he writes that the devil prowls around like a roaring lion, looking for someone to devour (1 Peter 5:8). The image is deliberate. A lion's roar induces fear, and not the healthy kind.

A lion rarely targets the strongest animal in the group. It looks for the one that has wandered away, the one that is distracted, injured, tired, or separated from the others. When that moment of vulnerability appears, the lion strikes with sudden force, knocking its prey down and clamping onto its throat until the animal can no longer breathe. Peter's choice of words is intentional. Satan actively hunts after us, and we must be alert. The Greek word translated *devour* carries the sense of swallowing something whole, consuming it completely. The picture is not merely of being wounded or harassed; it is also of being overwhelmed and pulled under, engulfed by a force that wants to suffocate a person's faith, hope, and strength until they feel they are drowning beneath the weight of darkness.

The apostle Paul addresses this issue in Ephesians. God's Word exhorts us to put on the full armor of God because the struggle we face is not merely human. *For we do not wrestle against flesh and blood, but against the rulers, against the authorities, against the cosmic powers over this present darkness, against the spiritual forces of evil in the heavenly places* (Ephesians 6:12 ESV). There is a deeper conflict unfolding beneath the surface of our lives, and at times it can be downright unbearable.

Now, let me address something for a moment. Over the years, I have noticed two extremes that often appear within the body of Messiah when it comes to this subject. On one side are people who deeply believe in God and in the truth of the Word, but they rarely acknowledge the reality of spiritual opposition. For them, the Enemy is almost an afterthought, something theoretical rather than something active. On the other side are those who see the devil behind every inconvenience of daily life. If they catch a cold, they rebuke the devil. If their car does not start, they rebuke the devil again. Some people would probably rebuke a nasal drip. Neither extreme is particularly helpful or biblical, for that matter. What we need is balance. We must worship in spirit *and* truth, just like Jesus told the Samaritan woman at the well.

This is heavy teaching, and I understand that. But as a rabbi, I want to speak honestly about what was happening in those nights. Even after all my years of walking with God, after decades of faith and ministry, those long, dark nights in the hospital became a place where the Evil One began whispering into my mind. When you go that long without sleep, your mind starts to get foggy. You cannot think clearly. And that is exactly when the adversary likes to move in.

You want to know what Satan whispered to me? The first thing he said was straight to the point: "You're going to die. This is the end of your life."

After a while, the whispers became more specific. "After you die, your wife is going to meet someone else who will treat her much better than you ever did. Before long, you'll be nothing more than a memory and an afterthought."

Now, if I had been in my right mind, I would have recognized immediately how ridiculous that was. Nobody could treat my wife better than I do. I love that woman with all my heart.

However, the Enemy was after my mind and emotions when

I was at my weakest. There is a reason Jesus called Satan *the father of lies* (John 8:44). Deception is his native language. He whispers things that sound believable in the moment, especially when you are exhausted and afraid. After that, he went after something even more painful.

My children.

"You're going to leave them without a father," the voice whispered. "You're going to make life hard for them, and there's nothing you can do about it."

That one cut deep. I know exactly what it feels like to lose a father. I know the emptiness it leaves behind. And the Enemy knew it too. That is how he works. He studies the deepest wounds in our lives and then turns them into weapons, using them to pierce our hearts when we are most vulnerable.

The most personal attack came next.

Satan started whispering lies about my relationship with God. The voice suggested that the Lord had abandoned me. He said the Lord had stepped aside when I needed Him most.

And I will tell you something honestly. There was a moment in that hospital room, in the middle of the night, when the pain was unbearable, and the darkness felt heavy, that I found myself praying something from the deepest part of my heart. *"Lord, where are You?"* I cried out like a son who needed his Heavenly Father.

I said to Him, "God, I've tried my best in this lifetime. I don't know how good it was, but it was my absolute best. I've tried to serve You. I've tried to tell people about You. I went to all the countries You asked me to go to. And here I am, lying in this room in pain, wondering if I'm about to die, and You're nowhere to be found." By that point, my entire spirit had been crushed.

Here's the thing – God never asks us to pretend that evil does not exist. Scripture makes it clear that spiritual warfare is real, but it also teaches us that the Enemy is *not* sovereign.

He is *not* everywhere, and he is certainly *not* in control. God's Word opens our eyes to it so we are not caught unaware. The only way to find your way out from under the lies of the Enemy is through the truth of God. The apostle Paul says the belt of truth is the first piece of the armor of God (Ephesians 6:14). In a Roman soldier's armor, the belt held everything together. Without it, the rest of the armor could not function. In the same way, the Spirit of truth holds a believer together when life begins to shake. When you walk through seasons of pain, suffering, confusion, or testing, God's truth is what keeps you standing. The message of the gospel is not meant to leave us afraid; it is meant to leave us confident. Jesus Himself told His disciples that in this world they would have trouble – but to take heart, because He has already overcome the world (John 16:33). The Enemy is real. His attacks are real. But he does not get the final word. King Jesus does.

I want to pause here and say something important that is worth repeating: sickness, hardship, and suffering do not mean you have done something wrong. The point I am making is that one of Satan's tactics is to use hardship to erode our confidence in Jesus. In 2 Corinthians 4:16 (ESV, NIV), Paul reminds us not to *lose heart.* He is in the midst of his own suffering and says, *Though outwardly we are wasting away, yet inwardly we are being renewed day by day.* In other words, even as we suffer outwardly, God is still at work within us. Discouragement is one of the Enemy's most effective strategies. When a person believes that God is absent, indifferent, or finished with them, hope erodes, and the Enemy steals our trust in Him.

In John 10, Jesus is speaking within earshot of the Pharisees after they had cast a man born blind out of the synagogue. In response, He begins teaching about shepherds and sheep, exposing the difference between those who truly care for God's people and those who exploit them. In the middle of that teaching, He makes a statement that cuts to the heart of spiritual warfare: *"The thief comes only to steal and kill and destroy. I came that they may have life and have it abundantly"* (John 10:10 ESV).

Notice that the first word Jesus uses to describe the thief's work is *steal*. There is a reason for that. A thief rarely announces himself. He takes something subtly before you even realize it is gone. Once hope, peace, or confidence in God is stolen from a person's heart, the rest of the Enemy's work becomes much easier.

Satan wants us to believe in divine betrayal. His goal is to make you think that God has somehow kicked you to the curb and abandoned you when you needed Him most. The adversary loves to plant that thought in the mind, especially when a person is weak, exhausted, and in pain. That lie rarely arrives during the bright moments of life. It shows up in the dark. It shows up at three o'clock in the morning in a hospital room. It whispers when the machines are beeping and the pain will not let you sleep. It prowls and taunts when you are too tired to fight back.

I learned that lesson the hard way when I was fifteen years old. That was the year the thief came to steal the only life I had ever known.

JUST A BOY FROM THE BRONX

I was born in January of 1959 to Jewish parents in the Bronx, New York. When I describe it now, I sometimes jokingly call it the "garden spot of the universe," but anyone who knew the Bronx in those days understands the humor in that phrase. This was not the Bronx that later generations would see romanticized in movies or on television. It was raw, crowded, loud, dangerous, and often unforgiving. It was the kind of place that taught you early that the world could be a hard place to navigate.

My parents both came from deep roots in European Jewry.

My father's family had come from Germany, while my mother's lineage traced back to Austria and Poland. Like many Jewish families of that generation, our European family history was woven with stories of survival and hardship.

My father, Meyer, was not what most people imagine when they think of a typical Jewish dad. Many of the Jewish men I encountered later in life were highly educated professionals like doctors, lawyers, and accountants. They were often mild-mannered men who approached life and discipline with a steady reserve.

My father was cut from a very different cloth.

He was shaped by two of the most brutal forces a generation could face: the Great Depression and World War II. When the Depression struck in 1929, my father was only ten years old. Like millions of families across America, his family suddenly found themselves fighting just to survive. Childhood did not last long for boys in those circumstances. When his own father died, my dad was forced to become a man quickly. He carried responsibilities far earlier than a young boy ever should, helping to care for his younger brother and sister during years when survival required sacrifice from everyone. Then came the war.

At twenty years old, my father volunteered for the United States Army and became an Army Ranger during World War II. Rangers were not sent to the easy assignments. They were sent into the most dangerous situations imaginable. My father earned the Bronze Star for bravery in combat. He received the Purple Heart after being wounded by a grenade. At one point during the war, he was even listed as missing in action. Many men returned from that war broken in ways that never fully healed. My father came home standing with one arm mangled by a grenade and a mind rattled by what he had seen.

He carried the strength and discipline of a soldier for the rest of his life. But he was not a complicated man in the way people might expect. He believed in simple things: hard work, responsibility, and taking care of your family. Dad worked for the United States Postal Service at a major distribution facility in Queens. His days were spent sorting and loading parcels for delivery across the region. It was repetitive work, the kind that required endurance more than creativity, but it provided for a wife and four children, and that was enough for him.

My mother, on the other hand, had a very different personality. She had been raised much more deeply in Jewish tradition. The synagogue and the rhythms of Jewish life mattered deeply to her. She spoke Yiddish often, especially when she wanted to emphasize something, and she carried within her a deep sense of compassion for others. She began her career as a social worker in Harlem, and later became a schoolteacher in the South Bronx. She taught kindergarten, shaping the minds and hearts of children just beginning their journey through life. Even decades later, many of her former students remember her because she poured herself into her work with remarkable dedication.

My mother insisted that our family maintain a connection to Jewish life and the synagogue. My father went along with it mostly for her sake. Mom said he never particularly enjoyed attending services, but he showed up faithfully because it mattered to her. We lived in a low-income housing project at the intersection of White Plains Road and Gun Hill Road, a place known as the Gun Hill Projects. Six tall buildings rose into the sky, each twelve stories high. By the 1970s, many Jewish families had already moved out of the Bronx and into the suburbs as their economic fortunes improved. Our family was not among them. We remained in the projects, along with many elderly Jewish residents who stayed because their fixed incomes made moving impossible. Looking back as an adult, I recall that the buildings looked almost like prison towers. But as a child, I simply saw it as home. And within that home were some of the most meaningful moments of my childhood.

Tuesday nights belonged to my father and me.

My mother was working toward her master's degree during those years, so after finishing her job, she would leave in the evening for classes. While she was gone, my father and I developed a routine that became sacred to me. We would walk together through the neighborhood to a small Chinese restaurant not far from our building. It was nothing fancy, just a modest place where a father and son could sit down together in the middle of an ordinary week and share a meal. At the time, it felt like nothing special. Looking back now, I realize how special those ordinary moments truly were.

After dinner, we would walk home together along the Bronx sidewalks. Somewhere along the way, one of us would glance at the other and smile.

Then one of us would shout, "Race you!"

And just like that, we would take off running down the sidewalk like two kids. My father always won, every single time. I can still see him running ahead of me, strong and steady, full of life. To a boy, a father like that becomes more than just a parent; he becomes your protector, your shield, the person who makes the world feel safe. When my father was in the room, I felt completely secure. Nothing in the world seemed powerful enough to get past him to reach me. I loved him more deeply than I had the words to express. Life had also turned a corner, because after all those years of hard work, my dad had finally reached retirement. We would now enjoy spending happy, carefree days with him, now that he no longer had to work – or so we thought.

One thing I am profoundly grateful for is a simple habit I had as a child. Every night before going to bed, I would hug my father and kiss him good night on the cheek. It was our routine. I never went to sleep without doing it. Even today, I can still remember the rough feel of his whiskers against my lips.

The night he died, I did exactly what I had always done. I hugged him and kissed him good night. Then I went to bed. Life felt completely normal. It was the last time I would ever see my father alive.

I was fifteen years old. It was 1974. My three older sisters had already grown up and moved out of the house, so it was just my mother, my father, and me living in the apartment. Sometime during the night, while I was asleep down the hallway, my father stopped breathing. I woke suddenly to the sound of my mother screaming. At first, I thought I must be dreaming. Kids have nightmares, and for a moment, I tried to convince myself that was all this was. But the sound did not fade the way dreams do. It grew louder, more desperate, more real. There was something raw in it, something *visceral,* like the cry of a wounded animal struck deep. In that moment, even before I understood what had happened, I knew something in our world had just been shattered.

I ran down the hallway into my parents' bedroom. My father was lying still in the bed. My mother was beside herself with grief. I stood there in the doorway, and something inside me fell apart in a way that has never completely healed. The final image I have of my father is one that has stayed with me for decades. Two men came and placed his body into a large black bag. I stood there watching as they carried my beloved father out of our apartment.

And just like that, my hero was gone.

When you lose your father at fifteen years old, you do not yet have the language to understand what has happened to you. It is more than grief. It feels as if something structural in your life has suddenly been removed. Overnight, I felt exposed, as though I was standing in the open without the protection I had always known. For years, I described that loss as if I had lost a limb. Something essential had been ripped from my life, and nothing ever felt quite the same again.

Looking back now, I can see that something else was planted in me that night. A belief began to settle into my heart that sorrow and suffering were somehow woven into the pattern of my life. Loss had come so suddenly and completely that part of me began to expect hardship as a normal companion. It was the first time I became aware of darkness in a way that would stay with me for the rest of my life.

That loss shaped something else in me as well. It changed the kind of father I was determined to become. When your dad disappears from your life in a single night, something breaks in you that never fully heals. You learn, earlier than any child should, that the people you love can suddenly be gone. I carried that knowledge with me every day as I raised my own children. It lived in the back of my mind like a bruise you forget about until something presses on it.

So when I found myself facing that moment decades later, the fear that struck me hardest was not about dying; it was about them, my children. I knew exactly what it meant to be the one left behind. I had lived it. And the thought of my children standing in that same doorway, staring into that same kind of emptiness, was the one thing I could not make peace with.

My mind began racing ahead to the moments I might never see. I thought about their weddings. I thought about the day they might hold their own children in their arms for the first time. I thought about the milestones and celebrations that make up a life. More than anything, I wanted to watch my children flourish and become who God created them to be. I wanted to sit with them as adults, share wisdom, and walk beside them as a father through the various seasons of their lives. Those were the thoughts filling my mind.

When you lose someone close, you learn something about grief that people rarely talk about. The hardest moments are not always the painful ones. Sometimes the saddest moments are the joyful ones. There were many times when something good happened in my life, and my first instinct was to pick up the phone and call my father. I wanted to share the moment with him. Then I would remember that he was not there anymore.

That is the strange ache of loss. The joy arrives, but the person you want to celebrate with is gone.

Of course, none of us can predict the future. My children have already experienced many beautiful moments in their lives, and I am grateful for every one of them. What weighed on my heart was the desire to be there for *more* memories. I wanted to be there for the milestones that still lay ahead, to stand beside them as a father, to celebrate the goodness of God in their lives, and to share those moments when life is full and joyful.

WHEN THE HEART STOPS BEATING

Back in that hospital room, the nights kept coming. One night, around two o'clock in the morning, I had finally drifted off when the door opened, and a nurse came in to draw blood. I looked at her through half-open eyes and said, "Can I have your address?"

She stopped. "Why?"

"So I can come to your house at two o'clock in the morning and wake you up!" She looked at me for a moment and then we laughed. And I will tell you, even that tiny moment reminded me I was still a person. Still human. Still in the fight.

But the humor could only carry me so far.

The days at Emory began to blur together. Morning would come, but it never really felt like a new day. It felt more like a continuation of the same long ordeal, another stretch of hours marked by pain, uncertainty, and the steady parade of tests, scans, blood draws, specialists, and bad news. Every day, I hoped someone would finally walk into my room with clarity. Every day seemed to bring only more questions.

By late afternoon one day, they wheeled me downstairs for a CT scan with contrast. By that point, I was exhausted in every sense of the word. They had done so many tests and little procedures that I felt less like a person and more like a case file being passed from one department to another. I remember being moved onto the table and slid into the machine. I remember the cold, the sterile light, the strange stillness of those moments when you are alone with your thoughts and your fear.

Then everything went silent.

When I came to, faces were hovering over me. A *lot* of faces. Doctors. Nurses. Technicians. Everyone looked panicked, sweaty, and shaken. I remember blinking up at them and thinking, *What now?*

I asked what was going on, and one of them said, "Greg, can you hear me?" I said, "Yes." Then they told me I had coded. For two minutes, my heart stopped beating, and they had to revive me. I just stared at them. At that point, so much had already gone wrong that I could barely process one more thing. My first thought was not noble or spiritual. It was simply this: *You have got to be kidding me!*

I wish I could tell you that after that, the tide turned, but it did not. If anything, the sense of danger in the room only deepened. They brought me back upstairs, and by then it was clear that whatever was happening inside my body was bigger than anyone had first hoped. The scans still were not giving them the full picture. There was blood where it should not have been. There was pain no one could explain. And there I was, lying in the middle of it all, trying to make sense of a body that seemed to be turning against me piece by piece.

That is one of the strangest parts of severe illness. At first, you think of yourself as a patient. Then, after enough tests, enough bad reports, enough specialists standing over your bed with furrowed brows, you begin to feel more like a mystery no one can quite solve. I was not just sick; I was becoming a problem to be figured out. Every hour seemed to bring a new theory, a new concern, a new possibility worse than the one before it. By then, I had already spent so much time around hospitals and endured so many surgeries that I knew the look on a doctor's face when things were not going well. I had seen it before. I saw it again that day.

They moved me into the ICU, and the room changed. Everything felt more solemn there, more final. Even the air seemed heavier. People do not get moved into intensive care because things are improving. They get moved there because something is very wrong.

That night, the door opened, and Dr. Peter H'Doubler walked in. He is one of the best surgeons in the field, with more than forty years of experience, and he serves as Chief of the Vascular Surgery Section at Emory Saint Joseph's Hospital. I have known him for years, long enough that there was no need for niceties between us. He did not come in with false optimism; he came in with the truth.

Dr. H'Doubler told me they had no choice. They were going to have to open me up completely. He did not yet know everything they would find, but he suspected it was going to be very bad. He explained how complex cases like mine carry a high risk. I tried to lighten the moment the way I often do when the tension gets too thick. I asked him, half joking, if I should call my children and say goodbye.

He did not smile. He looked at me with a seriousness that cut straight through the atmosphere and said, "Yes; if it were me, I would."

There are moments in life when fear stops being an abstraction and becomes a physical presence in the room. That was one of them. Up until then, I had been living inside pain, confusion, and bad news. But this was different. This was the first moment I truly understood that I might not survive what was coming next. I prepared myself to make the phone calls to each child. It was already midnight, but it had to be done.

I called my oldest son first. His name is Jeremy. I became a father later in life, at thirty-five, and for five years, he was our only child. When Jeremy was little, he was my shadow. Wherever I went, he wanted to be there. We wore the same clothes sometimes. He wanted to be like me in every way. When you are a father, you hope your children will respect you. But when your son looks at you like you are the greatest man in the world, that is a feeling you never forget. When he answered the phone, I told him the truth.

"Jeremy," I said, "the doctors are about to open me up for surgery. They aren't giving me very good odds."

He didn't want to hear it. "Don't say that, Dad."

But I needed him to hear me.

So I told him what had been sitting in my heart. "Jeremy, listen to me. You never once disappointed me. Not one day. Not once. When I was with you, I felt ten feet tall. I felt like the luckiest father in the world." I meant every single word. There are memories a man carries that no one else sees. Moments with your child that stay buried deep inside your heart. That's what I was thinking about while I spoke to him.

"Some of my favorite times in life were the times I spent with you," I told him. Then I asked him for one thing. "Promise me something, kid. Stay close to God. Promise me you'll stay close to God."

He was quiet for a moment, and then he said something that broke me.

"Dad, if you don't make it, I'm not going to believe you're gone. I won't go to your funeral. I'm just going to pretend you're in another room somewhere and that you stepped out. And one day you're going to come back out. I don't want to imagine a world without you."

Then I called my daughter Shaina in New York. She is one of the toughest people I know. She doesn't cry easily. She's strong, composed, and steady. But when I told her what was happening, she broke. She began wailing in a way I had never heard before. "Dad, that's the worst news you could ever tell me."

I tried to calm her down, but I also wanted her to hear what was on my heart. "Shaina," I said, "do you realize something? I never had to discipline you. Not once. You were always so respectful to your mother and me."

It's a rare thing for a parent to be able to say that. "You are talented. You are compassionate. You have a beautiful heart. Please don't ever change."

My precious daughter was crying so hard she could barely speak. My heart was crushed into a thousand pieces because I love her so much. We said goodbye through sobs.

My son Max was there with me. I looked at him and told him how proud I was of the man he had become. I told him about the strength and integrity I saw in him, the qualities that made him who he was. And then he said something I will never forget. "Dad, everybody at the synagogue loves you because you're their rabbi."

He paused. "But what you don't understand is, you're *my* rabbi." Then he looked at me and said through tears, "So Rabbi, what am I supposed to do without my rabbi?"

My time with Maxie during that season was a gift I will always cherish. He stayed with me for hours every day and never wanted to leave. Each day, he drove from Macon to Atlanta and then back again at night. With traffic, it was about a two-hour journey each way. Still, he showed up and never complained. At night, just before heading out, he would pause at the door and look back, and our eyes would meet across the room. There was something in that connection a father never forgets. It was loyalty. It was love. It was the promise of a son determined to stand watch for as long as he could.

When I think back on those days, I realize that what he gave me in that hospital room was a gift that cannot be measured. He gave me his presence. And when a man is lying in a hospital bed fighting for his life, presence becomes one of the most sacred gifts in the world.

Then I spoke to my youngest, Lily. She is sunshine. She wakes up laughing, and she goes to bed laughing. She loves people. She doesn't have a cruel bone in her body. She's an athlete, an artist, and one of the most compassionate people I've ever known. I told her how proud I was of her, how beautiful her heart was, how much joy she had brought into my life.

She was crying. "Dad," she said, "this can't be happening."

Then she said something that cut straight through me. "You're my best friend. What am I supposed to do without my best friend?"

After the calls to my children, I was emotionally and mentally fatigued. It was the worst night of my life. And yet, even in that darkness, there was still hope, still goodness breaking through. People from Beth Yeshua International and from all over the world were praying for me. Some went to the Wall we had built at our congregation and stayed there for hours, crying out to God on my behalf. They fasted and interceded for my life and for my family. I will come back to that later because it deserves more space than I can give it here.

During those early days in the hospital, before my life-altering surgery, there was one person I found myself waiting for each day more than anyone else.

Bernadette.

I would watch the clock all night long until it hit eight o'clock in the morning, because that was when she usually arrived. In a place where the nights felt endless and the darkness pressed in from every side, that hour became holy to me. Eight o'clock meant Bernadette was coming through that door.

She has a kind of faith that I cannot fully explain. All of us who belong to the Lord have saving faith. But Scripture also speaks of a special gift of faith given by the Spirit (1 Corinthians 12:9). That is what Bernadette carries. It is a supernatural ability to believe when everything in the natural realm says the opposite. The Spirit empowers some people to look fear in the face without flinching and still say, "God is going to move."

We see that kind of faith throughout the Bible. Joshua and Caleb carried it when the rest of Israel trembled before the giants. The woman with the issue of blood carried it when she reached out to touch the hem of Jesus's garment. And the Roman centurion showed it when he believed that Jesus could heal his servant with nothing more than a word. Some people panic when the room is filled with bad news. Bernadette does not. Her strength somehow holds the whole room together. She steadies the people around her. And I can tell you from experience that when your own strength is gone, being near someone with that kind of faith is like standing near a fire when you are freezing to death.

I am a blessed man that God picked her as my wife. She prayed for me night and day. She sat beside my bed and strengthened me when I was too weak to even grasp at hope. She would tell me, "You're going to get better, and you're going to walk out of here." She said it with such conviction that even when my mind was under siege, some part of me still wanted to believe her.

And then there was her humor.

One morning, after a particularly brutal night, I had not

slept at all. I lay there staring at the clock for hours, waiting for eight o'clock, because eight o'clock was my sunshine. Bernadette would come in, open the drapes, wipe down my face, and for a few minutes, the room did not feel quite so miserable. But that morning, eight o'clock came and went. Then nine o'clock. And when you are that sick and running on no sleep, your mind starts going places it should not go. I started to worry about her. I was waiting for her. Finally, the door opened.

Bernadette did not just walk into the room. She practically waltzed in, smiling like she had just scored some kind of major victory. Now, I have been married to this woman for a long time. I know her. I am observant, very observant. I can tell when she is wearing a new outfit before she even says a word. And Bernadette, well, Bernadette has never met a store she didn't like. So I looked at her and said, "Are those new jeans and a new sweater?"

"Yes!" she said, with that childlike enthusiasm of hers.

I jokingly replied, "So I'm in here dying, and you went shopping at the mall!?" She looked at me like I had completely missed the point. "I did not go to the mall. I got them at the hospital gift shop."

I just stared at her. "The hospital gift shop? Seriously?"

Without missing a beat, she shot back, "Greg, it was seventy percent off!"

She's a special one. She was my advocate, my companion, and my strength when my own had completely run out. She rubbed my feet. She prayed for me. She sat beside me and refused to give in to despair. She stayed when lesser people would have folded. She stayed when there was nothing glamorous about staying. She stayed when the days were long, the nights were worse, and the outcome was uncertain.

Lying in that hospital bed, I began to understand the true meaning of love in a deeper way than I ever had before. Love shows up. Love doesn't look away. Love doesn't walk away. Love indebts itself. Love stays.

And Bernadette stayed.

DEEP CALLS TO DEEP

In Psalm 42, the psalmist records a line that mirrors my time in the hospital: *Deep calls to deep in the roar of your waterfalls; all your waves and breakers have swept over me* (Psalm 42:7 NIV). These were not words born from comfort, but from a place of deep distress. The writer was cut off from the place of worship, surrounded by voices that mocked him and questioned where his God had gone. His world had become a storm, wave after wave crashing in, leaving no space to breathe.

If you have ever stood under a waterfall, even a small one, you know what that feels like. The force of the water does not fall gently; it pounds down on you. The weight of it pushes against your chest and shoulders. The sound is so loud that it drowns out every other noise around you. You cannot stand there for long before the pressure becomes overwhelming. That is the picture Psalm 42 gives us. One wave crashes down, and before you have even caught your breath, another one follows. Then another. Deep calling to deep. Wave after wave breaking over your head.

That was exactly how those nights in the hospital felt. Crises did not come one at a time. They came in succession, one crashing down on top of the next. *Infection. Kidney failure. Dialysis. The relentless pain. The inconclusive tests. Coding in the CT scanner. The prospect of not making it through a necessary, major surgery.* Each new report felt like another breaker rolling over me before I could recover from the last one.

But even in the roar of the waterfall, the writer did not stop speaking to God. And somewhere beneath the noise of the machines, beneath the fear and the pain, I realized something important. The waves were real. The pressure was real. The darkness of that night was real. But so was my God.

After telling my family how much I loved them, I turned my attention to Jesus. I thanked Him for the life He had given me. I thanked Him for allowing me to serve His people. And I especially thanked Him for the greatest privilege of all – that I was His son. I asked God to watch over my family. I asked the Holy Spirit to guide the surgeons who would soon hold my life in their hands. And I asked Him to give me peace with whatever the next day would bring.

Truth be told, I was not optimistic at all. I had been hearing one bad report after another, and everything around me felt dark. I was walking through the valley of the shadow of death, and the light had all but disappeared.

At five o'clock the next morning, the nurses arrived to prepare me for surgery. They wheeled me toward the operating room.

I took a deep breath and placed my life in the hands of the only One who could save it.

> *Fear not, for I am with you; be not dismayed, for I am your God; I will strengthen you, I will help you, I will uphold you with my righteous right hand.*
> —Isaiah 41:10 (ESV)

– CHAPTER FOUR –

THE GREAT PHYSICIAN

THE MORNING OF THE SURGERY DIDN'T ARRIVE WITH SUNSHINE. It arrived with a heaviness that pressed against the windowless walls of my room, a gray and colorless morning that only a hospital can produce. I lay propped on thin pillows, a sheet pulled across my weathered body, staring at the ceiling the way a man does when he has run out of things to bargain with. The room smelled of antiseptic and pain.

I had been through countless surgeries before. There is a version of you that shows up in the operating room after the seventh or eighth time that acts like it knows the drill, like it has developed some kind of armor. But I want to be honest with you: that armor is thinner than it looks. And that morning, lying there waiting for the five o'clock crew to come through my door, I did not think I was going to make it. I really thought this might be the last morning I ever saw on earth.

The doctors knew something was wrong, but they could not yet see clearly enough to understand what they were about to face. There was no scan, no test, no image that could fully explain what was happening inside my body. My surgeon, Dr. Peter H'Doubler, had sat with me and had spoken plainly. The only way forward was to open me up completely and search for the source of the bleeding once he was inside.

By that point, the pain had been building for days, steadily intensifying, until it was no longer something I could ignore or push through. I knew my body was in serious trouble. There are moments when you stop negotiating with reality, when something deep within you recognizes the truth before anyone says it out loud. This was one of those moments.

And yet, at the same time, I knew exactly where I stood with God. I am not afraid of what comes after death. The reality of seeing Jesus face-to-face someday is a promise I press on toward. There is a kind of assurance that settles deep within the soul when you truly know Him, not just in word, but in truth.

Still, even with that assurance, something inside of me resisted.

I was not ready to die.

It was not fear of eternity. It was the quiet, undeniable sense that my time here was not yet finished, that there was still work entrusted to me, earthly responsibilities that had not been completed. Most of all, I wanted more time with my family.

IT'S ALREADY DECIDED

A nurse stepped into the room before dawn and reached for my wrist to check my band. Name, date of birth, patient number. Greg Hershberg. I was still me. At that particular moment, I wished I was someone else. She moved with the efficient calm of someone who has done this a thousand times before, preparing me for transport, adjusting things at the bedside, speaking in that steady hospital voice that tries to keep everything from becoming too real. But fear does not care how calmly someone speaks to you. Fear has its own language, and by then I knew it well.

Before they wheeled me away, Bernadette and the kids arrived.

My wife did not come in with fear. She carried faith and conviction. She pulled a chair up beside my bed and took my hand, and she looked at me the way she has always looked at me across all the years of our marriage, with that calm and settled certainty that has carried me more times than I can count or properly repay. I tried to keep it light, the way I always do when the tension gets thick, and I said to her, "You know they're about to cut me wide open, right?"

She gently replied, "I know."

"And you're not scared?" I asked.

She looked at me steadily and said, "Greg, God didn't bring you through all of this just to let you die. You are going to make it."

I am telling you that in that moment, my wife was doing the preaching, and I was the one sitting in the pew. There is no pride in saying that. There is only gratitude. Because when your own faith has been worn to its absolute thinnest, God in His mercy will sometimes place someone right beside you whose faith has not weakened. Bernadette was that person for me that morning. She was Aaron and Hur at the hill in Exodus 17, holding up the arms of a man who no longer had the strength to hold them himself, standing firm so that the battle could still be won.

She held my hand and prayed for me, speaking straight to our Heavenly Father. There is life and death in the power of the tongue, and Bernadette understands this better than anyone. When she finished, she looked at me and said it again, steady and certain, "You're walking out of here. It's already decided."

TWELVE AND A HALF HOURS

They came for me not long after. Nurses released the brakes on my bed and began to move me toward the door. I looked back at my family as they pushed me into the hallway. Through blurred tears, we locked eyes, and in that silent exchange, we said everything we did not have the strength to put into words. I want you to know something about a moment like that. You stop thinking about the big things. You stop thinking about ministry and legacy and all the things you built. You just think about your family's faces. You think about how much you love them and how much they love you, and you think, *Lord, please. Just please. Please give us more time together.*

Now, let me explain what was actually about to happen in that operating room, because if you do not have a medical background, this surgery means very little to you, and I want you to understand the weight of it. The miracle to come only makes sense once you understand the mess.

My aorta had been compromised. The aorta is the main artery that carries blood from your heart through the center of your body. It is the largest blood vessel you have, the main highway for everything your heart is trying to deliver. And in my case, that highway was shredding at a terrifying speed.

An old stent inside my aorta had ruptured. On top of that, a staph infection in my bloodstream had already begun eating away at the surrounding tissue. The damage was not isolated. It had spread into the aorta and into the iliac arteries – the vessels that branch off and carry blood down into your legs. And here is what made my situation so serious. The vessels were not just damaged, they were *infected.* In medical terms, that changes everything.

When an artery is damaged, it can sometimes be repaired. But when it becomes infected, it cannot simply be fixed. It has to be removed entirely. That was the reality I was facing. In my case, seven stents inside my aorta and iliac arteries had become infected. Because stents become embedded within the artery itself, they cannot be removed on their own. The infection had spread to the surrounding vessels, leaving no other option but to remove the affected arteries altogether.

The procedure I was scheduled for is called an axillary bifemoral bypass. It is neither common nor simple. In basic terms, Dr. H'Doubler would take an artery near my armpit and connect it to the arteries in my groin. He would run a synthetic tube beneath my skin, creating a new path for blood to flow to the lower half of my body and rerouting it around the infected area.

This is the kind of surgery you only do when there are no other options left.

What no one could fully see before opening me up was that the rupture had not stayed contained. It had broken through into my small intestine, into a section called the jejunum, and I was bleeding internally in a way no one on the outside could detect. Once they got me on the operating table and discovered that, everything changed. Damaged sections had to be removed in real time. I lost a tremendous amount of blood, and the team had to adjust on the fly.

Dr. H'Doubler is a renowned surgeon and one of the best in the business. He told me afterward that he had never performed that exact surgery before under those circumstances. I asked him how he knew what to do. He said he had to go back to his foundations, back to his training, back to the very beginning of what he knew, and think it through in real time. He stood over my body and figured it out step-by-step with precision and skill. The surgery lasted twelve and a half hours, which is absolutely nuts.

I have no memory of those hours, only what was told to me afterward, piece by piece. But one thing is clear: what happened in that operating room cannot be explained by medicine alone.

THE HAND OF THE LORD

At first, the surgery began as might have been expected. But it soon became a battle between life and death.

Dr. H'Doubler later told me there were a few moments during the operation when I had lost nearly all the blood in my body. The team was pumping blood into me as fast as they could, and it was pouring right back out. I lost twelve units of blood; the average person has about eight units. Both times, he looked up at the monitors and expected to see a flatline. He told me he was preparing himself to walk into the waiting room and tell my family it was over.

But somehow, by the grace of God, my heart kept beating.

There was no blood left to sustain it. There was no clinical explanation for why my heart continued to beat. When he told me this later, I asked him the only question that came to mind: "How does a heart keep beating when all the blood is gone?" You cannot drive a car without gas.

Dr. H'Doubler is a careful and precise man, trained his entire career to deal in facts and measurable outcomes. He did not have a medical answer for me. What had happened on that table, in his own assessment, could not be explained by anything he had been trained to explain. He described it simply as a *phenomenon.*

I knew what it was. It was a miracle. The Great Physician had arrived. *Adonai Rapha* had stepped into that operating room. God was there in the hands of a surgeon who stayed when he could have walked away. He was there in a heart that kept beating when, by every natural measure, there was nothing left to sustain it.

In our modern language, we tend to use the word *miracle* very loosely. We say things like, "It was a miracle I got a good parking spot," or, "It was a miracle that it all worked out in our favor." And I want you to hear me, because this matters. That is not how the Bible speaks. In the language of Scripture, we do not speak casually about miracles, because a miracle is not a matter of convenience. It is not luck. It is not even what we would call a blessing in the ordinary sense. A miracle is when the natural order itself yields to the authority of Heaven, when the Holy One, blessed be He, reaches in and does what no human hand could ever accomplish.

This is what the Scriptures call the *Yad Adonai,* the hand of the Lord. When Israel stood at the sea, they did not say, "How fortunate!" Instead, they saw His *mighty hand* (Exodus 14:31 NIV), and they understood that God Himself had stepped into their situation. And when His *mighty hand* moves, it leaves behind more than relief. It leaves a testimony. It marks a life in such a way that you can never go back to explaining things the way you once did, because you know, *deep within you,* that God intervened.

That is what I believe happened to me.

There are moments, even now, when I have visions that I cannot fully explain. It is as if I am brought back into that operating room, and I see the Lord standing over me. He is engaged. His hands are upon me, sustaining what should have failed, pumping life back into my heart. And I am left with the unshakable knowledge that what took place on that table was not merely medical intervention. It was the hand of God.

Why did I not die? I still don't have an answer. As Paul writes, *"For who has known the mind of the Lord, or who has been his counselor?"* (Romans 11:34 ESV). There are places where the human mind simply cannot go, where we are invited to stand in awe rather than demand explanation. God is God. Miracles will never fit neatly within our understanding. They do not follow the limits of what we expect or what we can explain. They reveal the majesty of the Most High, which our minds cannot fully comprehend.

During my surgery, my family remained in the waiting room, praying and believing. The weight of not knowing the outcome is its own kind of suffering, a kind that presses on you with every passing minute. However, they were not alone. People from all over the world were praying. Friends, family, and members of our community lifted my name before the Lord. At Beth Yeshua, people even fasted forty days, each person taking a day, standing in the gap and crying out to God on my behalf.

My surgeon, Dr. H'Doubler, is highly respected in his field. He's also very handsome and well put together. But when he finally stepped out of the operating room, my son Max told me afterward what he saw, and I have never forgotten it. "Dad," he explained, "it looked like he had been in a war!"

Later, I asked Dr. H'Doubler why he stayed and kept working on me when all hope was lost. "I couldn't give up on you," he said. "I just *had* to keep going." He felt compelled even when the odds were stacked against us.

That was the Lord moving in a man who did not even know it. That is what God does. He does not only work through the people who believe in Him, but He also works through whoever is willing to stay at the table when everything says to walk away. He worked through a surgeon's hands and kept a heart beating with no blood to beat with. When it was all over, Dr. H'Doubler said it had been an honor to do my surgery. An *honor.* After decades of saving lives, after everything he had seen and done, he called my surgery an honor. I wept when he said that. I am not ashamed to admit it.

Now I need to say something here, and I want you to hear my heart. I know there are people with *very* strong faith, *way* stronger than mine, who have walked into operating rooms and not come out. I know families who have prayed just as hard, believed just as deeply, and still lost someone they loved. Cancer has taken people who loved God. Children have died in the arms of parents who trusted Him completely. So when I tell you my story, I do so carefully. I don't fully understand why I'm here and someone else is not. I've had to wrestle with that.

All I know is that the same God who was with me in that operating room is the same God who is present in the rooms where the miracle doesn't come the way we hoped. He does not leave. He does not turn away. Whether in healing or in loss, He is still God, and He is still near. The same God who sustained me in that room is the same God who sits with people in their grief. His presence is not dependent on the outcome. He is there in the miracle, and He is there in the mourning.

When I finally came back to the world after my surgery, I was in the ICU, and three days had passed. The pain was unlike anything I can properly describe. It was deep and overwhelming, the result of something catastrophic that my system was still trying to process. When I eventually got a look at the incision running down my torso, I thought I looked like Frankenstein. I had been opened up and put back together, and it wasn't pretty. I felt vulnerable, weird, and exposed.

But I was alive, and I am forever grateful.

When I reflect back on that time, I was not strong, and I was not full of faith; I felt like I was being *carried.* It is often there, in that place of weakness, that the grace of God does its deepest work. Today, I stand in absolute awe of the way Jesus uses even medical professionals to impact our lives through the work of their hands. Nehemiah once prayed, *But now, O God, strengthen my hands* (Nehemiah 6:9 ESV). How often do we overlook a prayer like that? How often do we forget that God is not only concerned with our hearts and our faith, but also with the work of our hands, the very places where we are called to serve and help others?

In the weeks after my surgery, I hugged and thanked all the nurses and doctors. Some of them were crying, others were smiling, and a few just shook their heads like they still could not quite believe what they had witnessed. Even from the hospital bed in my mangled, post-surgical state, I continued to love and pray for them. The Holy Spirit also gave me words of knowledge to speak into their hearts.

What stayed with me long after that moment was this: not all of us will stand in an operating room or hold someone's life in our hands the way they did – but every one of us has been entrusted with something that *matters.* The work of your hands carries purpose. It matters when you pray. It matters when you speak to someone who is losing hope. It matters when you prepare meals for your children. It matters when you use your creative gifts to impact this generation.

Sometimes, when we walk through hardship, we feel forgotten, or we struggle to understand what God is doing. But hear me, beloved: *The LORD is near to the brokenhearted and saves the crushed in spirit* (Psalm 34:18 ESV). In Hebrew, the word *near* means "close enough to touch." Jesus is not far from you in your pain. His presence is most powerful in the places you feel shattered. He loves you so very much.

Now, I want to pause here and let two men share their perspective on my medical crisis. Dr. Daniel Robitshek and Dr. Lawrence Kirk are close friends who stood with my family through those hospital days and anchored us in the storm. Their words matter because they speak as both physicians and as men who love me. There is something powerful about hearing from people who watched it all unfold and can say, "I was there. I saw it. And I cannot explain it apart from God."

TESTIMONY: DR. DANIEL ROBITSHEK

The vascular surgeon confirmed that surgery was indeed the only option for Greg and that it needed to be performed as soon as possible. The surgeon advised that it carried with it a greater than fifty percent mortality risk, possibly much greater. The next twelve hours leading up to the surgery were some of the most emotional for all of us who knew and loved him, but nothing compared to what Greg and his family had to consider.

The next morning came, and he was transported to surgery. The wait was awful. One hour became two, which became four, which became eight. At about the ten-hour mark, his beloved vascular surgeon came to speak with the family. He was obviously exhausted and nearly in tears. He narrated the ordeal of Greg losing more than twice his total body volume of blood, requiring the transfusion of an exhaustive number of units of multiple different blood products. He explained that on several occasions during the surgery, he thought Greg would surely not survive, that his heart would arrest.

But it never did. He recounted that he had to remove not only the eroded portion of the aorta and Greg's iliac arteries, but he had called in another surgeon to help remove also part of Greg's bowel. He stated several times that from a purely medical perspective, Greg was not out of the woods. And then – this elite physician and academician – stated unequivocally that it was a true miracle that Greg was alive.

TESTIMONY: DR. LAWRENCE KIRK

I am a family physician from Byron, Georgia. I have known the rabbi for over eight years, and during that time his teaching has profoundly shaped not only my understanding of Scripture, but also my personal walk with God. Because of the depth of that relationship, what unfolded next was not merely something I observed; it was also something that deeply affected me on both a personal and spiritual level.

As the rabbi's condition continued to deteriorate, he required an emergency surgery that essentially removed his aorta. I knew then that his chances of surviving were extremely low. I remember the surgery lasting many hours, and I remember praying as he was in the operating room, fully aware that the outcome was completely in God's hands.

As miraculous as his survival was, his recovery has been just as astonishing. Looking at him now, you might never know what he endured. Months later, when he sent me a picture of the removed aorta, it was hard not to reflect on the overwhelming odds he faced, from illness to surgery to recovery, and to see divine intervention at work.

While I cannot quantify his odds medically, what happened was far beyond what I believe could be explained by medicine alone. At the same time, I know that not every believer experiences this kind of outcome. I lost my own father to cancer at the age of sixty-six, and yet I believe God was just as present with my father as He was with the rabbi. This experience reminds me that as believers, we are never alone. God is with us in healing and in loss, in miracles and in mourning. And no matter the outcome, God is still God.

* * *

After my miracle surgery, I stayed eighteen more days at Emory before talking my way out of that hospital against every doctor's advice (my stubborn personality won that day). Still, I had a brief taste of freedom, including the moment my son drove me home and I pressed my face to the window like a man rediscovering the world. I will share all about it later, including what happened next when I nearly died yet again.

But first, I need to take you somewhere else entirely, because some of you have been sitting with a question that has nothing to do with surgery or staph infections or aortas. It is a more fundamental question than any of that. You might be wondering how a Jewish man from the Bronx, a man who had once walked away from God completely and *meant* it, ended up on an operating table trusting in the Lord Almighty. You might be wondering how a boy raised in a synagogue, who knew the Shema before he knew much of anything else, came to believe with everything in him that Jesus of Nazareth is the promised Messiah of Israel.

Those are *very* important questions, and they deserve real answers. The answer does not begin in a church. It does not begin with a street preacher, a television broadcast, or a dramatic vision in the night. It begins with two young newlyweds who had their hearts set on a honeymoon in Jamaica.

However, God had another plan. We packed our bags for Israel instead. And what happened next did not just change our lives. It *saved* them.

> *Many are the plans in the mind of a man, but it is the purpose of the Lord that will stand.*
> —Proverbs 19:21 (ESV)

– CHAPTER FIVE –

THE MOUNTAIN WAS CALLING MY NAME

BY THE TIME I WAS EIGHTEEN YEARS OLD, I WAS DONE BELIEVING IN GOD. After my father's death, my mother and I began to drift away from practicing our Jewish faith. We never joined another synagogue, but we did observe the High Holy Days. Beyond that, we gradually embraced a more secular lifestyle and eventually left the Bronx, settling in the suburbs of Yonkers, New York.

I threw myself into achievement, and on paper, I looked like a success story. I graduated high school with honors, attended college on scholarship, graduated *magna cum laude,* and landed a job with Arthur Andersen. At the time, Arthur Andersen was one of the most prestigious accounting firms in the world and part of the Big Eight. Back then, just getting an interview there meant you were doing something right. Getting hired meant you had officially entered the world of adult respectability, with the suits, the hours, the pressure, and the unspoken promise that one day all of this would make you feel important. It certainly looked important. It also made me miserable.

I stayed there from 1980 to 1982, which in dog years was well over a decade. The work was torturous to me. I was chained to a desk, crunching numbers sixty hours a week, listening to a bunch of people mumbling corporate-speak all day. If you know me at all, you know this was not exactly a match made in Heaven. I had the attention span of a squirrel on espresso. Today, people would say, "Greg, you had ADHD." Back then, they just said, "Sit down and focus," which was about as effective as telling the wind to stop being windy. I was a social person trapped in a profession that required me to be an isolated human adding machine.

People sometimes ask why I chose accounting in the first place. The answer is less dramatic than you might think. I was mathematically inclined, I wanted security, and I had no real mentor helping me discern what I was actually made for. In my young mind, there were two respectable lanes: science or math, and math felt more manageable. So, I chose accounting. It seemed practical, stable, and respectable. What I did not know then was that the Lord, in His mercy, wastes nothing. Even my interest in numbers would later help me see patterns in Scripture and appreciate the order and brilliance of God's Word. But at the time, I was simply a young man trying to build a life that looked solid from the outside.

Then came the phone call that changed everything.

A recruiter reached out to me one day, as they often did in New York, looking for young professionals with Big Eight accounting experience. I told him, quite plainly, that I was done with accounting altogether. He laughed and told me to come in anyway. In the middle of the interview, he suddenly asked whether I had ever considered going into recruiting. I practically screamed yes before he finished the sentence.

That decision changed the whole trajectory of my life. For the first time, I found myself in a field that actually fit the way God had wired me, though I did not know enough then to say it that way. Recruiting had energy, movement, people, instinct, persuasion, and just enough razzle-dazzle to feed my ambition.

I took to it immediately. I rose quickly and became vice president in just a few short years. By the age of twenty-six, I was making six figures. Later, I co-founded my own firm, hired a team, and built a business that served major financial institutions. On the surface, it looked as though I had won in life and had become a major success story.

A big part of me actually loved it all. I had the luxury condominiums, the sports cars, the investments, the money in the bank. I had come a long way from where I started. My father had died with only a hundred dollars to his name, and much of my drive was aimed at making him proud. He had spent his life doing backbreaking work with little to show for it. Dad never made it out of the slums, and that reality shaped my entire outlook. So, walking into those high-rise buildings in my slick suit seemed like proof that I had survived and overcome it all. Somewhere inside, I was saying, "Look, Dad, I made it! I became somebody. You must be so proud!"

My dad used to tell me that I had the potential to become the first Jewish president of the United States. After I was named president of my own company, there was a part of me that laughed and thought, "Well, there you have it! A nice Jewish boy *did* become president!" It was my own little joke, but there was an ache hiding under it. Humor does that sometimes. It smiles while the soul limps.

Despite all my success, something was unmistakably missing. I carried a heavy emptiness that, at times, felt like a suffocating cloak. I did not have the language for my pain. Success can give you options, but it cannot give you wholeness. It can furnish a beautiful apartment while leaving the heart completely empty. It can put a man in expensive shoes while he has no true vision. I had money, travel, women's attention, status, a physique I was proud of, and a future that people envied. And yet, beneath it all was a hunger I could never satisfy.

At the core, I was idolizing self and things, something people have struggled with from the very beginning of time. Idols are people, places, or things we turn to for meaning, identity, or fulfillment apart from God. If I could go back and speak to that younger version of myself, or to anyone who finds themselves chasing validation in the same way, I would say this: none of it will ever quench the gigantic God-sized hole we all carry. Success and power simply cannot touch the longing we all have for our Heavenly Father.

During the rise of my career, I did what many people who are both wounded and successful do. I went looking for spirituality in places that allowed *me* to remain in control. I turned to Eastern philosophy, New Age ideas, martial arts disciplines, Transcendental Meditation, and a patchwork of borrowed beliefs that flattered my ego while starving my soul. I was not looking for repentance. I was looking for enlightenment. I wanted transcendence without surrender. That kind of spirituality can make a man feel deep while he is actually becoming more deceived.

By 1985, I had become heavily immersed in martial arts, not just physically but also spiritually. I found a teacher who was gifted, charismatic, and convincing, and like many charismatic leaders, he pretended to be rare, elevated, and indispensable. I was his top student. We trained for hours and then spent more time immersed in spiritual teachings around the practice. We read Eastern religious texts, meditated, and moved deeper into what I now recognize as not merely a discipline, but also a kind of cultic web.

I thought I was ascending. Looking back, I see I was getting lost in the attic of my own intellect. There was a whole lot of *self* in me during that season, which is why I work so hard now as a rabbi to help people understand their true identity in Jesus. Otherwise, we end up looking for fulfillment in all the wrong places.

One night, I walked into a gym where a friend of mine worked. Behind the desk stood this stunning young woman with long dark hair, piercing blue eyes, and enough beauty to make a man forget what he had come there to do in the first place.

I was talking with my friend near the counter when he asked if I wanted to use his condo in Florida sometime. I said I would love to, but I did not have anyone to go with. Without missing a beat, the young woman behind the desk jumped in and said, "How long do I have to pack my bag?" She was beautiful, yes, but she was also quick-witted, and for me that combination was powerful. I asked her out that very night.

Her name was Bernadette.

When we met, I was twenty-five, and she was eighteen. Yet in many ways, she had seen more of life than I had. She was strong, independent, and already carrying burdens that had forced her to grow up quickly. Her father had died young, and by sixteen, she was supporting herself. Bernadette had been raised Roman Catholic in the Bronx, attended Catholic school, and learned early how to navigate life on her own. After her father passed away, her mother met a man who lived upstate and begged her to come with them. Bernadette refused. Instead, she stayed in the Bronx with her sister and pursued a career in acting and modeling while working as a personal trainer in New York City. That's how I met her.

We came from different worlds, yet carried strangely similar wounds. Grief has a way of recognizing grief in others. We started dating, although I wasn't interested in marriage. I wanted companionship, but mostly on my own terms.

On our second date, I drove to pick her up, and her neighborhood was so rough that I didn't even want to get out of the car. Mind you, at the time I was a workout maniac, so physically I could hold my own. But this was different. Her area was downright dangerous. Bernadette had moved in with a divorced woman who had three kids. I had what I can only describe now as a *savior* complex, so I said to her, "I don't know if we will keep dating or not, but I can't let you live where you are living. I've got to get you out of here."

Not long after that, she moved out, and from that point on, we stayed together.

We fell in love, but the relationship was rocky for a couple of reasons. First, we were both deeply involved in the social scene, living a very *secular* lifestyle. I loved to party and was usually the one people called when they wanted to go out. Drugs and alcohol were a normal part of life for my group of friends. In reflection, I can now see why this part of my story matters. It shows that no one is beyond God's reach. At the time, though, it all felt normal. It was simply how we lived.

Second, I was a very selfish man. I had a lot of growing up to do, and I can see that clearly now. Even so, I remember telling a friend that if I ever got married, Bernadette would be the one. In some way, my heart already knew.

We continued to date, and then something unexpected happened.

My martial arts teacher, of all people, began talking about the Bible and Jesus! That threw me off completely! Eastern philosophy and martial arts made sense to me. They belonged together in my mind. But *Jesus*? That felt bizarre, intrusive, and frankly, off-brand. In my understanding, Jesus belonged to somebody else's religion. We had nothing to do with Him. I thought He was basically the founder of Catholicism, or at the very least the headliner. I did not know He was Jewish. I did not know the New Covenant emerged from Jewish soil. I did not know that the promises of the Hebrew Scriptures were fulfilled in Jesus. I just knew He was not for us. Or so I thought.

I initially pulled away from the school because all the Jesus-talk felt weird to me. It rocked my emotional stability, and when

I left, I was deeply wounded and very insecure. I felt as though I was leaving my lifeline, which is how most environments like that are designed to make you feel. However, the teacher's influence on my life was so potent that I eventually returned. I decided it would be okay to read the Bible a little. Bernadette became involved as well, and before long, we were sitting in these exhaustive Tuesday night study sessions that went on for hours and hours.

Also, I should add a little context when it comes to Bernadette. She had grown up in a Catholic school, but she didn't really understand what it meant to know Jesus in a real and personal way. To her, God was more of a concept than a living reality. He was a religion instead of a relationship. In many ways, she was just like me. We were both searching for something – or rather *Someone* – we just didn't understand the pure gospel. We read Scripture with our teacher, but the interpretation was mixed together with elements of Hinduism and Buddhism. At the time, it sounded deep and thoughtful, but we did not yet have the discernment to recognize what was happening. Still, the Lord is so kind and merciful, and He used it all for a greater good. It just took us a while to get there.

One of the first Bible stories that really captured my attention was the transfiguration, which is found in Matthew, Mark, and Luke. In this account, Jesus takes three of His closest disciples – Peter, James, and John – up on a mountain to pray. There, before their eyes, Jesus is transfigured. His appearance changes, His glory is revealed, and standing with Him are Moses and Elijah.

This struck me deeply because, as a Jew, Moses and Elijah are not just names to us. They are *pillars* of our faith. They are *heroes.* They represent the Law and the Prophets, the very foundation of who we are as a people. So when I read that they were standing there with Jesus, it stopped me in my tracks. I remember thinking, *Why are they with Him in glory? What is that supposed to mean?*

Back then, I did not understand the deeper meaning, that they represented everything God had already revealed to Israel. I didn't realize that the Law and the Prophets had always been pointing to Jesus. Moses and Elijah were not there to share the spotlight; they were there to point to the Son. In Luke 9:31 (ESV), *[they] spoke of his departure, which he was about to accomplish at Jerusalem.* This reveals that the cross was not unfolding by chance, but was always part of God's redemptive plan.

When I first read the story, I did not grasp the fullness of the revelation, but something in me was compelled to know more. Little did I know that soon I would meet Jesus on that very same mountain, and my life would change forever.

I'll share one more brief story from when I first began reading the Bible. One day, I was sitting in my New York condo, studying the Gospel of John, when I came upon these unforgettable words that Jesus spoke: *"Do not let your hearts be troubled. You believe in God; believe also in me"* (John 14:1 NIV). As I read that verse, something in me broke open, and I began to weep uncontrollably. I couldn't explain it, and I certainly didn't understand it, but it seized my heart in a way I had never experienced before.

In that moment, I began to realize that the Word of God is living and active. I also had this overwhelming sense that Jesus was real and believable, but as a Jewish man, it was difficult for me to admit it. Even without a theological framework, the power of the Lord was already at work in me. Seeds were being planted.

After much time and reflection, here is what I now understand. The Shepherd really does leave the ninety-nine to go after the one. Jesus was coming after me. He was also coming after Bernadette. And He pursues all of His sheep with the same intention. First John 4:19 reminds us, *We love because he first loved us.* The overwhelming love of Jesus is impossible to put into words. His love is not distant or conditional. It is *personal.* It is *relentless,* and it knows no bounds.

As I reflect back on my life, I realize what it means to be like the Prodigal Son, the one who wandered and chased everything the world had to offer, only to find himself empty. I want you to notice the order of the parable. Before anything else, the son had to come to himself (Luke 15:17). That is the pattern for all of us. There comes a moment when the illusion breaks, and we finally see clearly where we are and who we have become. It is in that moment of clarity that our hearts begin to turn.

Then, while the son is still a long way off, the father sees him, runs to him, embraces him, and restores him. That is the kind of love God has for us. Earthly kings do not run, but our Father does. He does not stand at a distance waiting for us to get it right. He runs *toward* us. The parable is not ultimately about the lost son; it is really about the loving Father. And without realizing it at the time, I was ready to go to my Father.

THE ENCOUNTER

By the late 1980s, something in me had changed. I was thirty years old, financially successful, and for the first time in my adult life, I actually wanted to get married. So one evening I made dinner at my apartment, and I asked Bernadette to be my wife.

We were married on September 24, 1989, in Tarrytown, New York, overlooking the Hudson River. The ceremony was officiated by a colleague of mine who, as it turned out, was also a justice of the peace. The wedding was beautiful and the neutral ground allowed both our Jewish and Catholic families to be present. Twenty-four hours later, we were in a limousine on the way to JFK to catch a flight to Israel.

Now, let me be clear. Israel was not our first choice. We were Caribbean people. Give us white-sand beaches, warm water, tropical breezes, and a good meal, and we were more than satisfied. Israel, in our minds, was not exactly romantic. Jamaica was far more appealing at the time. And yet, looking back now, it's obvious that God was directing our choices. That's how the Holy Spirit works. What we often call coincidence is actually His providence unfolding.

In my autobiography, *From the Projects to the Palace: A Rags to Riches to True Riches Story,* I share more about the full arc of my life and how I came to know Jesus. But for the sake of this book, I'll focus on a few stories, including how we ended up choosing the Holy Land, and, more importantly, how we became Jesus followers.

The first thing that happened was that my martial arts teacher suggested that we should go to Israel for our honeymoon. Even though he was teaching a mixed bag of Bible study and Eastern religions, he spoke about Israel like it was an adventurous pilgrimage. At the time, I thought the idea was completely ridiculous. It made no sense to me, and I laughed it off. But the very next day, while riding the train into the city, something unusual happened. I found myself sitting next to a man who happened to be Jewish. That might not sound unusual, but this was a train where the same people sat in the same seats every day, and I had never seen him before.

We started talking, and during the conversation, he mentioned that his father-in-law owned a travel agency in Manhattan that specialized in trips to Israel. He told me that if I was ever interested in going, he could connect me.

When I got home, I told Bernadette about these back-to-back encounters. Instead of hesitating, she lit up and said we should actually go! We eventually met with the agent, though I still was not completely convinced. Even so, we decided to move forward, and he booked us a deluxe trip with the whole nine yards included. To give ourselves a little reassurance, we also planned a trip to the Greek Isles at the end of the journey, just to make sure we would have some fun on our honeymoon.

We flew into Tel Aviv and then caught a connecting flight down to Eilat, located at the southernmost tip of Israel on the northern edge of the Red Sea. Eilat sits nestled between the Sinai Mountain range, with Saudi Arabia visible in the distance. It is a resort town, a playground for Israelis, the way the Caribbean was for us. We felt right at home. We went scuba diving and water-skiing, enjoyed gourmet dinners, and danced late into the night.

After a few days there, we headed north to Jerusalem. I want to be transparent with you here – once we arrived, I was already missing Eilat. Jerusalem made us uncomfortable in a way I could not articulate at the time. I know now that Jerusalem carries more spiritual warfare over it than any city on earth. The Enemy is not passive about that city, and even a person with no theological background can feel the heaviness of that battle without knowing what to call it.

We toured the Old City, took in the historic sites, and after a couple of days, I mentioned to Bernadette that maybe we should drive up to the Sea of Galilee before we left. We only had two days remaining in Israel before we were off to Greece, and one of those would be a travel day. If we were going to make it north, we had one chance.

The next morning, we set out to rent a car. The office was closed for Rosh Hashanah and Yom Kippur. Let that sink in for a moment. I was in Israel, in the middle of the holiest season on the Jewish calendar, and I had no idea. That tells you everything you need to know about where I was spiritually at that point. One employee happened to be there, catching up on paperwork. When she saw my last name, Hershberg, she realized I was Jewish and showed us favor. It was the first time in my life that having *berg* at the end of my name had worked to my advantage.

So off we went to Galilee. Along the way, Bernadette and I picked up a few Israeli soldiers who were hitchhiking, which, in 1989, was not unusual. Soldiers thumbed rides to get around the country, and in a strange way, it added to the whole experience. It all seemed exciting and perfectly normal. There was something oddly reassuring about having an armed passenger in the car.

When we reached the Galilee region, we noticed another soldier standing by the roadside with his thumb out, waiting for a ride. We pulled over and asked if he spoke English, and he did. I leaned over and asked, "Do you know where the Mount of Transfiguration is?" Ever since reading that story in the Bible, something in me had been stirred with curiosity. He shook his head and said no, then asked if we would mind dropping him off at a place called Tabor. We told him we would, and he gave us directions as he climbed into the car.

We drove a short distance more, dropped him off, and then I looked to my left. I saw a stunning mountain, and it left me quietly undone in a way I couldn't explain.

It rose up out of the surrounding landscape with a kind of solitary majesty. If you've never been to Israel, I'll do my best to describe it. Mount Tabor sits apart from the surrounding land, and it's not jagged or pointy. It's almost dome-like, and that's what makes it so striking. When I saw it, my heart skipped a beat, and I'm not trying to be dramatic, that's just the truth. There was a pull I couldn't ignore. It was no longer just a mountain in front of me. It was as if something had reached down from the summit, fastened itself somewhere deep in my chest, and was drawing me in.

From there, I was a man on a mission. I jumped out before the car had fully stopped (while my beautiful new bride screamed at the top of her lungs), ran to the entrance gate, pushed through, and kept walking until I came to a basilica with a plaque on the wall.

"Basilica of the Transfiguration."

My knees buckled. It was the same mountain I had read about in Scripture, the very place where Jesus was transfigured! *I was standing on it.* Only later did I realize that Mount Tabor and the Mount of Transfiguration were one and the same. I just didn't realize it when we set out that morning.

Suddenly, I heard a voice say, "Come away with me and pray."

I wanted to respond, but I was at a complete loss. I am embarrassed to admit it, but I did not know how to pray. Everything I had learned up to that point was rooted in Eastern philosophy and meditation. So, I did the only thing I knew. I found a quiet garden area off to the side, climbed up onto a three-tiered rock formation, closed my eyes, and tried to empty my thoughts.

And then it happened.

With my eyes closed, I began to see what I can only describe as a vision, like a film playing on the inside of my eyelids. I saw the eastern sky open. Not like clouds parting, but like a veil being torn from top to bottom. A figure of a man came through the opening as the veil was being pulled back. His face shone like the sun. His clothes were as white as light. He emerged from the sky and pressed Himself against me, chest-to-chest, face-to-face. He looked like a typical Israeli man with dark features.

Jesus spoke directly into my ear. He told me He loved me. He told me that, yes, He was the One I had been reading about. He told me He was going to prepare a place for me and that He would come back for me. All I had to do was believe that He was the promised Messiah.

I believed Him. There was no part of me that doubted.

At that moment, something in me broke open. A wellspring rose from deep within my soul, and His love overcame me. I wept like a child longing for his Father. I could not stop, and I did not try. Looking back now, I do not believe it was a cry of pain or even a cry of joy. It was something else entirely. It was a sanctifying cry. The Lord was beginning to empty me of myself as I was being filled with Him. He was cleaning the house from the inside out, and apparently, there was a whole lot to clean.

When Bernadette found me sobbing, she asked what was wrong. I told her I had just met God! She later said her first reaction was confusion. She thought, "How did I miss Him? I was right here!"

Her moment was coming though. She just didn't know it yet.

Before we left, I asked Jesus one question I couldn't walk away without asking. I said, "Now that I believe You are the prophesied Messiah, I guess I have to stop being Jewish and give up Judaism, right?"

His answer came back immediately. "Why? *I* didn't!"

I did not fully understand that answer yet. At that moment, I thought I must be the only Jewish person in the universe who believes in Jesus, so now what do I do? What do I call myself, and where do I go from here? As a young man, there was absolutely no mention of Jesus in my synagogue, in my household, among my Gentile friends, or in my life at all. We had nothing against Him per se; we just had nothing to do with Him. I was trying to figure it all out.

Now, some of you reading this might be wondering, if I didn't really believe in the one true God, how was I still Jewish? And that's something important to address. You see, I was raised in an Orthodox synagogue. Although my family didn't strictly practice Orthodox Judaism, we went to synagogue every Shabbat, and I attended Hebrew school twice a week. I was dedicated to the Lord at birth, given my Hebrew name, circumcised on the eighth day, and bar mitzvahed in the temple at age thirteen. Until my father died, I tried, in my own way, to live according to the tenets of the faith. By the way, I failed miserably.

I didn't know God well because intimacy with the Lord was never something we talked about in Hebrew school. I knew of

Him through external religious practices, but I did not know Him *personally.*

Judaism is unique in that while it is one of the three major religions of the world, alongside Christianity and Islam, it is also a kind of nationality. It's an identity of people. So when I was young, and someone asked me my nationality, I would say without hesitation, "I'm Jewish." My friends might say Italian, Spanish, or Irish, but for me, it was always the same answer. So even though I wasn't practicing my faith at the time, I was still, in every sense, one hundred percent Jewish.

As we drove down the mountain, I kept turning these thoughts over in my mind, trying to make sense of what I had just experienced with Jesus. Then, as we drove south, we saw a sign that read: "CAPERNAUM, THE TOWN OF JESUS." We decided to stop.

Capernaum, known in Hebrew as *Kafar Nachum,* means "Village of Comfort." This was not just another historical site. This was where Jesus lived for a time and carried out much of His ministry. It was here that He taught in the synagogue, healed the man with the unclean spirit (Mark 1:21-28), and where a paralyzed man was lowered through the roof so he could be healed (Mark 2:1-12). There are many places in Israel where the exact location is uncertain, but this is not one of them. Capernaum's coordinates are absolutely and unequivocally known.

When we arrived, we found the entrance gated and operated by Franciscan monks. They had strict rules, and we were denied entry because we were not modestly dressed. We were wearing shorts, and our knees were exposed. That was enough to keep us out. However, something in me would not let it go. I approached the priest at the gate and tried to reason with him, even asking if he believed the Lord was truly concerned with our clothing. He stood firm. The rules were the rules. We walked away frustrated, brokenhearted, and dejected. This was our last day in Israel, and we didn't know if we would ever return.

And then, just as we were heading back to the car, something extraordinary happened. The priest suddenly whistled and waved us back. He held up two pairs of work pants with ropes to use as belts. We were going in! We ran back, grabbed the clothes, changed as quickly as we could, and made our way inside with our odd new clothing. If there had been social media back then, this would have been one of those moments that went viral.

The village itself was small. We walked through the remains until we came upon a first-century synagogue, and it drew us in immediately. It was simple, yet there was something deeply moving about the place where Jesus had ministered. Standing there, I knew we were on holy ground.

As I took it all in, the stillness was suddenly broken by the sound of knees hitting the ground, followed by loud wailing. I turned and saw my wife on her face in the synagogue, crying her little heart out.

When she finally came to, she told me what she had seen. She had a vision of the synagogue in the first century, filled with people dressed in the clothing of that time, and she was sitting among them. Jesus was moving through the room, stopping to pray for different individuals. When He reached her, He placed His hand on her and said, "Be healed."

Bernadette had always wanted to become a doctor, but her circumstances had never allowed it. So the Great Physician came to her instead. He met her there, in that village of comfort. It is still hard to put into words. Even now, I can see that entire day so clearly in my memory, and it brings tears to my eyes.

Needless to say, our lives were changed forever on the trip. We left New York as secular newlyweds with no real faith to speak of. Eighteen days later, we returned home as entirely new people.

Here's something I often share when I tell this part of the

story. At the time, I didn't understand the indwelling and power of the Holy Spirit. I met Jesus on that mountain, and the encounter was very real. But what I didn't yet understand was that His presence was not confined to a place. I believed, at that point, that if I left Mount Tabor, I might somehow leave Him behind.

Looking back now, I can see why the Lord met me the way He did. He knew where my life was headed. He knew I would one day teach His Word and help others understand who He is. And because of that, Jesus made it unmistakably real for me. He met me in a way I could never deny, never explain away, and never forget.

But here's the truth: We don't have to go to Israel to meet Jesus.

The same God who met me on a mountain in Galilee meets people every day, right where they are. He meets them in moments of mourning, in moments of celebration, in prison cells, in hospital rooms, in bedrooms and bathrooms, and even in their cars. Why? Because Jesus comes to us. And not only does He meet us where we are at, He stays with us. The Spirit of God takes up residence in the heart of every believer.

Jesus told the disciples, as He prepared to depart, "*Nevertheless, I tell you the truth: it is to your advantage that I go away, for if I do not go away, the Helper will not come to you. But if I go, I will send him to you*" (John 16:7 ESV). That same promise remains for us today.

STEPPING INTO PUBLIC MINISTRY

When I came home from Israel, I did what I always do – I went all in. I've always been an all-or-nothing guy. That's just how God wired me.

I quit my job and turned the company over to my partner. I started telling everyone I encountered about Jesus. *Everyone.*

Remember how I excelled in my recruiting career? Well, now I was recruiting for the Kingdom, and I took the job seriously! I shared about the Messiah with the person on the elevator, at the deli counter, and anywhere a human being made eye contact with me. Even living in New York felt purposeful because there were so many people to talk to! I was ready to share the gospel with anyone and everyone who would listen.

I also discovered something remarkable. I had struggled with reading comprehension my whole life. However, when I opened the Bible, something was different. The words made sense. More than that, they felt *alive,* like each sentence had its own heartbeat. For the first time in my life, I was not getting through a book, the book was getting through me!

Now I need to speak about something important for a moment. When Bernadette and I returned home, there was a lot in our lives that needed to be purified. The sanctification process was long and difficult, as it is for every believer. We can be delivered from Egypt, but it takes time for Egypt to get out of us. God is so patient and kind though. He does not rush our transformation. He is faithful to walk with us, step-by-step, as He forms us into His likeness.

In the first couple years of marriage, I felt like I was losing everything, including my hair. Bernadette and I both knew we could not go back to our old way of life, but we did not yet know how to fully walk in the new one. In time, we made the decision to leave New York and move to Florida to start fresh. We had no jobs and no friends, but we had Jesus, and somehow, we knew that would be enough.

It was in Florida that our son Jeremy was born, five years after we got married. He was our only child for five more years, and then we had three children in succession.

During that time, we joined a messianic congregation in Florida called Beth Judah, and our family grew close to a wonderful community of believers. Jesus was right. I didn't have to stop being Jewish. He was my Jewish Messiah, and I loved spending time with Him. During that season, Bernadette and I worked various jobs, but we lived a very simple life.

In the spring of 1999, about ten years after our trip to Israel, the Lord shook up our lives again.

The congregation we joined had gone through a very painful season. The rabbi stepped down due to improprieties and left. When a shepherd fails morally, the sheep scatter, and scatter they did. Many exited, including the worship team and the core families who had anchored the synagogue. All that was left was a wounded group of about twenty-five people. We had a mortgage and no one to lead us.

I asked Bernadette if we should look for somewhere else to attend. She looked at me and said, "I cleaned the toilets in this place. I am not going anywhere."

That settled it.

One day, the elders came to me and asked if I would step up as interim leader. Here's the truth: I had no formal training. I was not a rabbi. There is no seminary in the world churning out messianic rabbis in volume. We are a fledgling movement, and leaders do not emerge through programs, but through calling.

Interestingly enough, we see this pattern even in the first century. In the book of Acts, Peter and John stood before the religious leaders, speaking with a boldness that made no sense on paper. They were not formally trained men. These former fishermen had no credentials that would have impressed anyone in that room. And yet, they were the very men God used to help lay the foundation for the body of believers. Something about them was undeniable. Scripture says, *Now when they saw the boldness of Peter and John, and perceived that they were uneducated, common men, they were astonished. And they recognized that they had been with Jesus* (Acts 4:13 ESV).

Of course, I don't place myself alongside these titans, but I recognized a similar thread in my own journey. When we spend time with Jesus, our lives drastically change. In fact, I had felt something stirring since 1989, a sense that the Lord might one day use me in vocational ministry. But there is a difference between feeling called and actually stepping forward.

The ten years that followed my encounter with Jesus were not years of formal training. I didn't enroll in a seminary or follow a traditional path. Instead, I spent hours in the Lord's presence each day because I simply wanted to know Him. He had revealed Himself to me, and I couldn't get enough of Him. I love Jesus so much. I wanted to understand His heart, and even His feelings.

The Holy Spirit became my teacher, and the Scriptures that once felt difficult or distant began to open up to me. They came alive in a way I still can't fully explain. At times, I would even speak what I was learning, saying it out loud just to practice how I might one day teach others.

During that time, I was serving in small but purposeful ways. I led youth Bible studies, ministered in prisons, and sat with the older generation in nursing homes. Wherever there was an opportunity to share about Jesus, I was there. It wasn't structured or strategic; it was simply an overflow of what He was doing in me. I loved teaching about Him.

After the elders approached me about leading Beth Judah, I got on my bicycle. That had become my way of spending time with the Lord. I rode out to a quiet trail because I needed to hear from Him. I told Jesus plainly, "If this is You calling me, I'll do it. But if this is just men who need a warm body, I need You to tell me. I'm not doing this without You."

He told me something that day that I have never forgotten. He said that every roadblock I had ever hit when I tried to pursue ministry on my own had been placed there by Him.

God wanted me for Himself. He wanted someone who had not been shaped by an institution, someone who would simply do what He said. I had fulfilled my hidden season well, and now I was ready to lead others.

I rode home sobbing, talked to my wife, went back to the elders, and told them I had clearance.

From that small congregation in Florida, God eventually led us to Macon, Georgia. It was there that Beth Yeshua International was born, a place where Jew and Gentile worship together as one new man, just as Paul describes in Ephesians 2. For more than twenty years, we have had the extraordinary privilege of serving as senior leader. Our children grew up in that synagogue. But I want to be clear about something. What has taken place during this time is not something we could have built on our own. This is the Lord's doing.

What began as a simple yes to God has grown into a global messianic ministry focused on outreach, education, and caring for the poor. Today, we have more than two hundred congregations in India, as well as congregations in Kenya, Australia, Germany, Israel, and across the United States, along with ongoing mission work throughout Africa. The ministry now supports schools, orphanages, and local congregations, reaching people in ways we never could have imagined when this all began.

One of the more unique expressions of this work has been the establishment of a congregation inside Pulaski State Prison for women in Georgia. It is truly innovative. We hold weekly gatherings there, and three women from Beth Yeshua faithfully lead the services. In addition, we meet very practical needs.

The ministry started like this: many of the women there were not receiving basic toiletries such as feminine products, toothpaste, and shampoo. God highlighted the need, and we answered. We partnered with a grocery chain to secure these items at cost and now supply them on an ongoing basis. Along with that, we provide spiritual resources, including books and other materials, to support them in their faith journey.

All we did was say yes. God did the rest.

The boy from the Bronx who lost his father at fifteen, who chased success until it ran dry, and who stopped believing in God altogether, yes, *that guy* became a messianic rabbi. Ever since then, I have humbly stood before God's people, opened His Word, and done my best to point them to Jesus.

I have walked with my Redeemer through joy and through grief. Through seasons of abundance and seasons of absolute lack. Through the births of children and the deaths of people I loved. Through church splits and breakthroughs and everything in between. And through it all, one thing never changed: God was faithful. *Every single time.* He's never abandoned me.

I thought I understood what that meant. But then came the hospital room.

Lying there with tubes coming out of my body, fighting for my life, I finally understood David. Not the David who slayed giants, but the David who cried out in agony, *How long, O Lord? Will you forget me forever?* (Psalm 13:1 ESV).

How long?

That became my battle cry.

> *The night racks my bones, and the*
> *pain that gnaws me takes no rest.*
> —Job 30:17 (ESV)

– CHAPTER SIX –

BREAKING POINT

BEING ALIVE AND FEELING ALIVE ARE NOT THE SAME THING. Nobody prepares you for that until it becomes your reality. I had survived twelve and a half hours on an operating table. My heart kept beating when there was no blood left to sustain it. About seven inches of my aorta and my iliac arteries were removed from my body. By every reasonable measure, I should have been dead. And yet, here I was.

Alive, but only in the barest sense.

At this point, I had been in the hospital for several weeks. Thanksgiving had come and gone, and Hanukkah was on the horizon. Our planned cruise to Panama was not going to happen. You would think that waking up on the other side of life-threatening surgery would feel like victory. You would think gratitude would be topmost in your emotions. What nobody tells you is that the body does not process a miracle the way the soul does. In those early days, I was not celebrating anything. Helplessness settled in like an unwanted friend.

They say the eyes are the windows to the soul. If you had looked into mine, a hollow emptiness would have stared back. The light was gone. I did not look like a man who had just been preserved by God against all odds. I was no longer a rabbi empowering the people I had been entrusted with. I was not a father pouring love into my children or even a husband who could serve and do things for my wife. I was just a helpless man on a hospital bed who knew his identity in God, but didn't exactly feel it. I was withered down to dust and despair.

When I surfaced from whatever darkness the surgery had put me in, time had lost all meaning. There was no clear sense of whether it was morning or night, no real understanding of what had been done to me, only the crushing awareness of a man pushed far beyond his limits. The pain lay over me like wreckage, heavy and disorienting, with no relief. Days passed somewhere beyond my reach.

Moments of true rest came few and far between. I have always been a side-sleeper, but now I was on my back and confined in place. There was a sharp pull across my abdomen, a deep, tearing awareness that I had been opened and stitched back together. Tubes ran in and out of me, some taped to my skin, others disappearing beneath the sheets. I could feel them, foreign and invasive, reminding me with every small movement that I was no longer in control of my own body. I tried to shift, instinctively searching for some kind of relief, but I could not find any peace. I was tethered to the bed in discomfort.

Each day I had a date with dialysis, which was its own kind of education in humility. My kidneys had failed badly enough that I needed a machine to keep me alive. For three and a half hours, I would lie there watching my blood leave my body, pass through something mechanical, and return to my veins again. There is something about that process that strips away any remaining illusion of self-sufficiency. By the time each session ended, I felt completely empty and drained.

People kept coming through the room, checking and adjusting things, speaking in that calm hospital voice meant to make everything feel less serious than it was. I was deeply thankful for their care. But beneath it all, a steady agitation kept rising because I wanted to go home. I felt on edge, and it got worse by the day.

Do you know what the hardest question to answer is when you are sick? It sounds simple when it is asked, almost routine, something people say without thinking too deeply about it. But when you are the one lying in the bed, living inside a body that no longer feels predictable, it lands differently. It's complicated and foreign.

It goes like this: "Greg, how are you feeling today?"

On the surface, it seems straightforward. But the longer I sat with it, the more I realized there was nothing simple about it at all. Do you measure it by pain? Pain never really left. It only shifted, rising and falling depending on the medicine. Do you measure it by progress? The medical team celebrated small gains that did not feel like gains to me. Or do you measure it by something harder to name, like a broken spirit or even a little depression settling in?

If you say too much, they keep you longer. That reality settled in fast. So I learned to be deliberate. Each day became an exercise in restraint, sorting through what to share and what to hold back, trying to navigate my way out of a place I no longer wanted to be in. Self-control is a fruit of the Spirit, and mine grew by the day.

The real truth was complicated. I knew I was gravely ill. What I wanted was to rest and recover in my own environment, in my own bed, with the serenity of my house around me. I would dream about it the way a parched man dreams about water, lying there visualizing my own couch, imagining what it would feel like to fall asleep in the quiet without someone barging through the door. Eventually, I reached a breaking point and devised a plan to get out of there. My idea was to present myself as stable, strong, and moving in the right direction. Then I could go home.

When that did not work, I did the only thing I had left to do. I begged.

I called for my doctors, every one of them, and I looked them in the eye, and I said, "Listen. I know I'm probably not going to make it. But if that's true, I want to go home. I want to be with my family. I would rather die at home than in this bed. Please. Just sign me out."

One doctor looked at me like I had lost my mind, which was fair because in some ways I had, but I did not care. He said, "Greg, in good conscience, I cannot let you walk to your death. You still need dialysis every single day. Your body cannot sustain itself outside of this building."

He was right. I knew he was right. I could leave if I wanted, he told me. I could sign myself out of my own volition. But if I did, the insurance company would likely not cover my expenses, and by that point, the bill was probably sitting somewhere close to two million dollars. So that was out.

Every doctor I approached gave me a version of the same answer. The general surgeons said no. The nephrologists, the cardiologists, the pulmonologists, and the doctors from the Centers for Disease Control who had gotten involved in my case all said no. I hit a wall with every single one of them.

But here is the thing about a hardheaded guy from the Bronx with the gift of convincing. I know how to make a case, and I was not done making mine. Scripture talks about setting your face like flint. In other words, you dig in, and you do not budge. I figured this was as good a time as any to live that out.

When I got to the vascular surgeon, I approached him differently. This time, the move was not to talk my way out of it; the move was to show him.

What happened next, I will be honest with you, involved

a bit of a performance. The occupational therapist and the physical therapist came in to assess me, to see if I could stand on my own. So I pushed myself up against that bed in my little socks with the rubber grips on the bottom. My legs were shaking beneath my gown, and I fully expected to go tumbling down like a toddler. Everything in me wanted to give out, but somehow I stood. Then I walked. I wish I could say the Holy Spirit interceded, but I think it was just sheer stubbornness. For a brief second, I was highly impressed. Apparently the surgeon was, too.

He watched me for a long moment. Then he shook his head slowly, the way a man does when he knows he is about to do something he cannot fully justify.

"This goes against everything I know about medicine," he said, "but I'll sign it."

Before I left, one particular doctor came to find me. He was one of those who had been against my discharge from the beginning. When he walked into the room, he looked at me the way people do when they are genuinely scared for you and need you to know it. He said, "I love you. I am worried about you. I don't want anything to happen to you."

I looked at this doctor who had poured himself into keeping me alive through weeks of crisis, and I said, "I love you too."

Then we both just sat there with tears in our eyes. A doctor and his patient, two human beings doing their best to make it in this world, crying together, knowing the odds were against me. We both understood the gravity of the situation. Even then, I wanted to leave. I will never forget that moment as long as I live.

Before I go any further, I need to say something important. I went through a lot of darkness in that hospital, but that is not the full picture. God brought beauty into that place, too.

During those thirty days at Emory, something unexpected happened. I grew close to the people who cared for me – the nurses, the doctors, the custodians, and the staff who came and went at all hours. They cared for me physically, and in return, I did my best to care for them spiritually.

Somewhere between the checking and the adjusting, conversations would begin. They would talk about their lives, their families, the things weighing on them, and the things that brought them joy. I listened the way I always have. I prayed. I offered whatever encouragement I had to give. Again and again, God sent people into that room, and in those times, a lot of special moments took place.

Here's the thing: our love for Jesus and the call to make disciples of all nations does not stop when we are suffering. The church is not a building. We are the church. Even lying in that bed, I understood that I still carried a responsibility to love God's people and represent Him well. There were moments when I was worn down, moments when the long nights made me difficult to be around. But beneath it all, my love for people never left. I think they could feel that.

This is not a new concept. The apostle Paul showed us how this works. Even while imprisoned, he continued to teach, encourage, and love the people God placed in front of him. He wrote, *What has happened to me has really served to advance the gospel* (Philippians 1:12 ESV). His body was confined, but his calling was not.

At one point, Paul despaired of life itself because his suffering was very real (2 Corinthians 1:8). The same can be true in our lives. As believers, we do a disservice to others when we pretend that everything in life is rainbows and butterflies. Faith does not remove the weight of suffering; it anchors us in the middle of it. Through the power of the Holy Spirit, our weakness becomes the very place where God's glory is revealed (2 Corinthians 12:9). Even in the midst of pain and sorrow, our love for others must remain strong.

I lived this out in small ways. During my time at Emory, I gave away my books to anyone who asked, signing them right there from the hospital bed. There was something almost funny about it every time. I can still picture it: Someone leaning around the corner with a shy smile, asking, "Greg, do you have a book I can have?" I would invite them in, and before long, the room would shift. What started as a simple request would turn into something deeper, a real moment of human connection.

Other times, I would share the gospel directly to these distinguished and elite doctors. I used what little strength I had to lovingly proclaim the truth. When I was too weak to bring the sunshine myself, my family and friends brought warmth and kindness into the atmosphere. The fragrance of Heaven was poured out through the hospital corridors, and Jesus's love was always present.

Looking back, the season that stretched me to a breaking point became the very place where ministry mattered most. God has a way of using even our trauma to impact others, bringing glory and honor to Himself. So when the day finally came for me to leave, it was bittersweet for all of us.

Somewhere along the way, we had become like family.

Let me share something I have learned after decades of sitting with people in their hardest moments. When someone finally reaches a breaking point, it almost never looks the way you expect. It is not dramatic. It is not a tantrum. More often, it is firm and resolute. It comes after a long stretch of holding on with everything you have until, one day, you simply decide you are done.

I have seen it in people who stayed in the wrong job far too long. They kept showing up. They kept trying, until one day, they are simply done with it all. I have seen it in pastors who spent years pouring into others but were never replenished themselves. They eventually walk away from ministry and never look back. I have seen it in those fighting illnesses. They go through treatment after treatment. They keep pushing on. But over time, something in them wears down. They grow tired – *soul tired* – and they want to be done with it all.

The details are always different, but the feeling is the same. There comes a moment when there is nothing left to give, and the decision to be done is made. And strangely, there is often a sense of relief. Sometimes there is even a sense of anticipation and excitement.

That is exactly how I felt on December 23.

The nurse came in to prepare me for discharge and began helping me get dressed. My oldest son Jeremy stepped forward and said, "I can do it."

In that moment, my mind went back to all the mornings I had stood in his room when he was small, back when he could not yet dress himself. He would lift his little arms straight up, and I would pull his shirt down over his head, smooth it across his shoulders, and fix his collar. Then he would look up at me with those precious eyes, the way small children look at their fathers, as if you are their whole entire world.

Jeremy reached for the ties of my hospital gown and loosened them with steady hands. The fabric slipped away, and for a moment I felt exposed, not just physically, but in every way a man can be stripped down.

He lifted my shirt and gently guided it over my head, careful of every movement, as if he knew how fragile I had become. When my arms didn't quite cooperate, he waited. When I struggled, he adjusted. Not once did he make me feel like a burden.

Then he knelt. My son, whom I had once carried, now bent down in front of me and helped me step into my pants. He steadied me when I wobbled. He pulled them up slowly, making sure I was covered, making sure I was okay. And then he reached for my shoes. Piece by piece, quietly, carefully, my son dressed his broken father.

In that room, strength did not look like standing tall. It looked like a son kneeling low. Somewhere between the weight of his hands and the tenderness in his care, something inside me broke open – not from pain, but from the overwhelming realization that I was not alone in it.

Jeremy gave me something far greater than help. He gave me love. He gave me dignity. And I could not stop the tears if I had tried.

GOING HOME

The nurses loaded me up with twelve medications and arranged dialysis care for me back in Macon. The team settled me into a wheelchair and rolled me outside. The moment those doors opened, the fresh air reached me first. It felt like paradise.

Then the sun found me. It was December in Atlanta, but it happened to be one of those nice winter days that catches you off guard with how gentle it is. The light came down at an angle and landed on my face, and I closed my eyes and simply let it be.

Everywhere around me, I could hear the world just going on. Cars passing. People walking and talking. Wind dancing through the trees. Ordinary life continuing the way it always does, whether you are in it or not. The holiday lights caught my eye, and the whole scene felt almost cinematic, like something out of a movie, except it was real and it was my life. I have traveled all over this world. I have stood at the water's edge and witnessed sunsets painted by God. I have had many moments that brought great joy to my life. Not one of them touched the freedom I felt that day. All I wanted to do was spend time with my family and make up for lost time.

From the first day I sensed something was wrong, November 13, to the day I was wheeled out of those doors, December 23, forty days had passed. You do not need a seminary degree to recognize the weight of that number in Scripture. Forty days of testing. Forty days of stretching. Forty days of being stripped down to almost nothing.

I did not leave as the same man who went in.

NOT AGAIN

"Greg, Greg, can you hear me?"

The voice came to me from far away, as though it had to travel across water to reach me. At first, I could not place it. I could not place anything. There was only a strange heaviness, a thickness pressing against my mind, as if I were trying to wake up through layers of fog.

When I finally forced my eyes open, I saw Bernadette leaning over me. Her face was close to mine. There was concern in her expression.

"Greg, do you know where you are?"

I wanted to answer; I remember that much. I wanted to say something simple, something that would prove I was still myself, but I couldn't speak. My body felt foreign to me, like I had awakened inside someone else's broken frame. All I managed was the slightest shake of my head. "No."

"You're in the hospital," she said. Then she paused, as if even now the words required gentleness. "You've been on life support for seven days."

Seven days.

I thought I was dreaming.

The last thing I remember is being at home, sitting on the couch, wrapped in blankets because I could not get warm. I was still weak and fragile, still trying to recover from everything my body had been through, but I was home. We even took a family photo to mark the special occasion.

About five days after arriving, my oldest daughter Shaina

was with me on the couch. All of a sudden, I violently started coughing blood. She shouted for Bernadette.

My wife got on the phone with the hospital, and by the mercy of God, a doctor-friend of ours happened to be on shift that night. Providence is not always miraculous in appearance. Sometimes it looks like one person being exactly where they need to be at the exact moment they are needed.

She told him what was happening, and his response was immediate.

"Greg is in heart failure. His lungs are filling with fluid. You do not have much time to save his life. Get him here right now, and I will have a life-support machine waiting!"

Jeremy had just returned home, and he picked me up and threw me over his shoulders. They rushed me to the car and drove without hesitation, through lights, through traffic, through every obstacle that might have slowed them down. Later, I was told that if they had waited, if they had paused to do things neatly and properly, if they had chosen caution over urgency, I would not have survived.

By the time we arrived, my body was shutting down. I had congestive heart failure. There was no cushion left, no reserve, no hidden strength waiting to be tapped. I had reached the end of what my body could do. Every breath felt wrong. Shallow. Incomplete. Like my lungs could not fully open, no matter how hard I tried.

I was drowning in my own fluid.

The doctors moved quickly. Machines were connected. Orders were given. Decisions were made in seconds. The doctor had not exaggerated; there had been no time to waste. My kidneys had totally shut down due to the relentless strain of the last few weeks. I could feel everything accelerating around me while, at the same time, something inside me was slowing down. The voices that had been sharp and urgent began to fade at the edges, like they were moving farther and farther away.

My body, which had been fighting so hard to keep up, finally gave out. I didn't make a decision to let go; I just couldn't hold on anymore. And then everything went dark.

I was out an entire week of time before I finally opened my eyes again and realized I was still alive.

My son Max later shared an incredible story of what happened during that time. The staff noticed that whenever Bernadette walked into the room, my numbers shifted. My heart rate responded, and my oxygen levels spiked. Even when I couldn't speak, couldn't move, couldn't fight for myself, something in me still recognized her. Something in me still reacted to her voice and love.

Once I was removed from life support, they moved me to a local critical-care hospital. This is not a run-of-the-mill facility. It is built for people who have to learn how to be human again. That is the plainest way I know to say it.

It is where you relearn how to breathe, how to speak, how to swallow, how to eat, how to stand, how to walk, even how to think in a straight line. There are places in this world you never imagine seeing from the inside, and then one day you wake up and realize it's where you live. To be frank, many people do not come to a place like that on their way back to life. They arrive there on their way out of it.

Even now, when I write those words, I can still feel how unreal that season was. The new hospital felt like a borderland – not quite life as I had known it, not quite death – but some suspended place in between.

Time moved differently there. The body moved differently there. Even hope moved differently there. Things that had once been automatic were now monumental. A swallow. A word. A lifted arm. A moment of clear thought. Everything was difficult. Everything was measured.

And it was awful.

There is a temptation, when you tell a story later, to improve the wording, to sand down the roughness and find language that is more elegant than accurate. But I have no interest in doing that here. It was simply *awful.* By then, I was not doing well at all, and I learned something I had never known in quite that way before: There are levels of suffering. There are degrees of weakness you do not imagine until you meet them. Just when you think a human body cannot absorb one more blow, something else hits you. It is as if pain itself has dimensions, and illness keeps dragging you deeper through them.

Time began to lose its shape. Holidays passed without notice through that place. New Year's Day came and went in the hospital. The calendar kept moving as if life were unfolding normally somewhere else, but inside that room, it all flattened into one long stretch of endurance.

Days were marked less by dates than by medications, vital signs, therapy sessions, setbacks, and the exhausting effort of trying to hold on to yourself when so much of you seemed to be slipping away.

YOUR TIME IS NOW

On January 6, it was my sixty-fifth birthday.

That morning, Bernadette came into the room carrying the kind of brightness only she can carry. Some people have a natural ability to bring life into dark places. They do not deny the darkness, but they refuse to let it have the final word. She looked at me and said, "Happy birthday!"

I remember thinking with a kind of exhausted disbelief, *How exactly is this a happy birthday?*

God gave me a wife who knows me inside and out. She looked at me and answered the question I had not spoken aloud.

"Because you're alive."

That sentence stayed with me because it held both truth and tension. On the one hand, she was absolutely right. Life is life. Breath is breath. Another day is another day. If God grants you one more sunrise, that alone is not a small gift. But on the other hand, I was so depleted physically, emotionally, and spiritually, that gratitude did not come naturally to me at that moment. It is easy to praise the gift of life when life still feels recognizable. It is harder when you are alive in a way that feels stripped, diminished, and unrecognizable even to yourself.

My family had always known me as strong. Not perfect, but strong. A protector. A man who could carry things, lift things, move things, decide things, provide for others, and bear weight for people who needed him. I had been an athlete all my life. Strength was not just something I possessed – in many ways, my strength had become part of how I understood myself in the world.

From the time men are boys, so much of our identity is tied to that idea. Be strong. Get up. Push through. Provide. Perform. In the generation I grew up in, we were not taught how to properly accept weakness, and we certainly were not taught how to grieve the loss of strength when it happens. No one talks about the grief of growing older. The grief of becoming sick. The grief that comes when your body no longer responds the way it once did.

Even retirement, which is often seen as something to look forward to, carries its own kind of loss. You step away from a purpose and identity that has shaped so much of your life, and you have to learn how to live in a new way. When that loss of identity meets the failure of the body, it can be overwhelming. It is more than physical. It is deeply personal.

My family was now seeing me as a shell of the man I once was. Helpless. Dependent. Immobile. Needing assistance for the most basic acts of living. There is a humiliation that comes with that, and I do not use the word lightly. It is one thing to suffer. It is another thing to lose the dignity of being able to govern your own body.

Day after day, the darkness pressed in harder. Pain will do that if you let it. Weakness will do that. So will isolation. So will the long, repetitive indignities of being unable to do for yourself what you once did without thought. At some point, though I cannot tell you the exact hour, I had reached a place of finality.

That is the only word for it.

When that day came, I looked at Bernadette and asked, "Do you love me?"

After she said yes, I told her to take a pillow, put it over my face, and end it.

Those are terrible words to write. They are no easier to revisit now than they were to speak then. But they are the truth. I told her I had been a good husband. A good father. A good rabbi. I had done my best to please God. I had run my race as faithfully as I knew how. I wanted out. I wanted the nightmare to stop. If I could not have healing, then I wanted release. If I could not have strength, then I wanted at least some shred of dignity in the leaving.

Bernadette looked at me and did not miss a beat. "Greg," she said, "I don't look good in orange. I'm not sharing a prison cell with Large Marge."

Only my wife could answer the darkest sentence of my life with a line like that.

Bernadette would not let me quit. She believed life was worth living even when I was done. She saw beyond the room. Beyond the machines. Beyond the bed. Beyond the version of me that looked half-buried already. She held on to something I could not hold. Sometimes that is what love does. Sometimes the people who love us have to believe on our behalf when we are too shattered to produce belief of our own.

After my family left in the evening, things grew darker. And I do not mean only the room.

My frustration turned inward. My mind became a battlefield. I was having what I can only describe as a crisis of faith, and I think it is important to say that plainly because religious people are often tempted to tidy up these moments after the fact. We prefer stories where the faithful remain serenely faithful all the way through, where the dying saint whispers polished truths from a hospital bed and never once feels abandoned, angry, disoriented, or undone. But that is not my story. Pain has a way of exposing what is real. Suffering has a way of stripping theology down to the studs. It asks questions that cannot be answered with slogans.

There are mysteries too deep for neat explanations. There are nights so long that even a man who has preached, taught, counseled, and walked with God for decades can find himself whispering into the dark, *"Lord, are You here? Do You see this? Are You still with me in this? Where did You go? I need You now more than ever."* That is what happens when the soul is stretched to its limit and is still asked to endure more.

And then, in the middle of that dark season, on my sixty-fifth birthday, Bernadette walked in holding a blue balloon and a cupcake. She set them down and tucked a small gift into my hands. I tried to work at the wrapping paper, but my fingers refused to cooperate the way they used to. She helped me open the present.

Inside was a watch, inscribed with the words, *Now it's YOUR time.* In a moment when time felt like it was slipping away, she gave it back to me.

At first, I did not know what to do with that sentence. It felt too alive for the place I was in. Too forward-looking. Too prophetic, perhaps, for a man who at that moment could barely picture the next hour, much less some greater purpose ahead. But the words stayed with me. They lodged somewhere deeper than my conscious mind could reach.

Later, I asked her why she had chosen those words. She did not hesitate.

My wife declared that God was going to preserve me for something greater. She said this marked a moment. She said this was the time.

The time is now.

I have turned those words over in my mind many times since then. Not because they erased the suffering. They did not. Not because they instantly lifted me out of despair. They did not do that either. But because they came into the room like a declaration that my story was not ending where I thought it was ending. They contradicted the darkness. They stood against the lie that all that remained for me was diminishment and departure. They announced, before I could yet see it, that survival was not the same thing as conclusion.

On that day, we were supposed to be holding hands on a Panamanian cruise, stepping into our glory years with joy and expectation. Instead, there she was with a cupcake and a watch, handing me something far more costly. She was handing me hope.

I stayed in the hospital for a total of sixteen days that last time. By then, I had relearned how to walk, how to talk, how to lift my arms, even how to brush my teeth. I had lost forty pounds and felt like a fraction of the man I once was, stripped all the way down to something even more unrecognizable than before. But God, in His mercy, was not finished with me. He was patient enough to rebuild my life again, just not in the way I had known before.

I could share many more details from that final hospital stay. I could take you deeper into the nights, the setbacks, the prayers, the strange interior terrain a person walks through when he does not know whether he is moving toward life or toward death. But by now you understand enough to know what kind of season it was.

What I learned there, or perhaps what was burned into me there, is this: I came to know a level of pain I had never imagined, and a kind of sorrow that felt too heavy to carry. I learned what it means to be emptied out, not just physically, but in every way a person can be undone. And yet, alongside all of that, I encountered something deeper than the suffering. I experienced a love that held me in it. The love of God. The love of my family. The love of friends, elders, and people all over the world who prayed for me when I could not pray for myself.

Years earlier, at Beth Yeshua, we had built a prayer wall for the community. It was inspired by the Western Wall in Jerusalem, a place where people could come, write down their prayers, and bring them before the Lord. It stands nearly twenty feet high, but there is nothing inherently sacred about the structure itself. What mattered, what I believed then and still believe now, is that God meets people in those moments of sincerity. And He has, time and again.

Over the years, thousands have come to that wall carrying burdens they could no longer carry alone. Some arrived quietly, slipping folded pieces of paper into the cracks with trembling hands. Others came with urgency, writing prayers through tears, not knowing how else to put words to what they were facing. There were prayers for healing, for restoration, for prodigal children, for broken marriages, for provision when there seemed to be none. Some prayers were simple. Some were desperate. All of them were real.

During my medical crisis, that same wall became a place of intercession for me. Day after day, people came on my behalf. Some prayed for hours as I lay there fighting to breathe. One couple who I did not even think liked me stayed for four hours. Others shared my story across social media, and it was extraordinary to witness the power of unified prayer. My family truly felt strengthened during those days. I am forever grateful to have experienced that sense of community, and I will never downplay it.

Here's the truth: I wanted to return to life as I had known it. But when God answers a prayer for life, He does not always do it by handing you back the old life untouched. Sometimes He answers by taking you all the way through the valley and returning you changed. You're marked with a limp. That is what happened to me.

I did not come out of that season as the same man who entered it. How could I? A man does not lie helpless in the shadow of death, lose his strength, lose his certainty, lose his dignity, and then simply resume his life as if nothing happened.

Something in me had died there, and something else, by the grace of God, was born. So even today, when I hold that watch in my hand, I no longer see those four words as a birthday message. I hear them as a summons.

Now it's YOUR time.

Your time to live.

Your time to rejoice.

Your time to teach and proclaim the truth of the gospel.

Your time to reveal all the dimensions of Jesus that people rarely talk about.

Your time to record in a book all that you experienced.

Your time to become the man God is still forming.

That was the miracle I could not see in the moment.

I thought my life was ending.

It was really just beginning.

> *Jesus also did many other things. If they were all written down, I suppose the whole world could not contain the books that would be written.*
> —John 21:25 (NLT)

– CHAPTER SEVEN –

MARKED WITH A LIMP

WHEN THE HOSPITAL DOORS SWUNG OPEN TO RELEASE ME ON JANUARY 12, 2024, I DID NOT LEAVE AS THE MAN I HAD BEEN BEFORE. I crossed that threshold altered by suffering and grateful to be alive. They handed me a stack of discharge papers, stapled at the corner like an afterthought, and rolled me toward the light. I did not know if this was truly freedom or just a pause between battles.

Either way, I was going home.

The cold air met me first. Then the brightness of the day. After more than fifty days of hospitals, procedures, machines, intense rehab, and the long shadow of not knowing whether I would live or die, I was no longer confident of anything and dependent solely on God's mercy.

As I prepared to finish this final chapter, I found myself returning to that day again and again. It did not feel dramatic or triumphant. If anything, it was quite melancholy. But some days divide your life so completely that you do not understand their meaning until later. January 12 was one of those days.

I was alive yet very weak. My life still orbited around medications and dialysis appointments. My lungs were learning how to carry me again. I was discovering that survival and restoration are not the same thing. The distance between those two realities is where much of the real story lives.

As I began to reflect on the aftermath of my medical crisis, one question kept rising to the surface: *What have I actually learned?* There are many things – more than I can fit in here – but a few have stayed with me. I've learned that suffering doesn't leave you the way it found you. I've learned that healing rarely happens all at once. Some wounds close slowly, in layers, like scar tissue forming over time, and that's okay. I've learned that God can be present even in the seasons when He feels very far away, and that sometimes the deepest kind of faith is just putting one foot in front of the other. And most of all, *most of all,* I've learned that Jesus's love, patience, and kindness are far greater than we can ever fathom.

In many ways, the story of Jacob wrestling with God makes the most sense to me. We see a clear marker between his old and new life, and, as believers, spiritually, we all go through these kinds of seasons. I sure did.

When we find Jacob's story in Genesis 32, he is preparing to face something he has avoided for years. Jacob's past is catching up to him. He is about to meet his brother, Esau, the very man he deceived and fled from, and he has no idea how that encounter will unfold. So he does what many of us do when we are afraid: He makes a plan. He sends gifts. He tries to manage the outcome. But eventually, there is nothing left to control. Jacob had been a deceiver and manipulator his entire life, and the Lord was about to break every last thread of self-reliance and striving.

The Bible tells us that Jacob sent his family ahead of him, and by nightfall, he was left alone in the dark. And it is there, in that place of uncertainty, with his past behind him and his future still unknown, that everything changed. He wrestled with a Man through the night, and by daybreak, he walked away with a limp and a new name, Israel, because he had *"striven with God and with men, and [had] prevailed"* (see Genesis 32:24-28 ESV). Jacob did not overpower God. He endured. He remained. He held on through the darkness until the blessing came.

When the night was over, he walked away, marked forever with his hip wrenched out of place. In Hebrew thought, the hip is a place of strength, stability, and generational legacy. It is one of the strongest parts of the body, essential for walking, standing, and moving forward. So when the Lord touched him there, He marked the very place Jacob relied on for his own strength. The wounding became a visible sign of his encounter with God. There is a fascinating paradox here: the place of breaking often becomes the very place of new identity. He is broken and blessed at the same time.

Thankfully, Jacob's story did not end in the dirt, and neither did mine. Yes, physically, I have never been the same since my near-death experience. Some days I can hardly stand through an entire sermon. And yet I am more tender, more compassionate, and more humble. I love deeper. I teach about Jesus in a way that is only forged through long-suffering. When someone comes to me carrying grief or sickness or shame, I do not stand above it. I am able to step into the trenches with them because I know what it's like to be held by Jesus in the darkest parts of the night. That is the blessing I have come to see. I have seen the goodness of the Lord in the land of the living.

We all carry limps, and they become a key part of our testimony. They are not only for us, but also for the people who will one day walk a similar road. The real struggle is learning how to keep moving forward while still bearing the scars of the past. I'm still trying to figure it all out.

That is where my mind keeps going when I think about the last couple of years of my own life. I do not give up or lose heart. Though outwardly I am wasting away, inwardly I am being renewed day by day. I did not leave that hospital season as the same man who entered it. Something in me was stripped away. Something in me was confronted and chiseled down to dust. Something in me died.

And yet, by the grace of God, I am somehow still limping forward.

PRAY LIKE IT IS YOUR OWN

I've had the privilege of sharing the gospel on six continents, across remote villages and in towns I still cannot pronounce. Ever since I came to know Jesus, something in me has been drawn to tell people about Him. I don't mean that in a polished or religious way. I mean, I genuinely *love* it. I cannot keep quiet about who He is. When you love Someone so much, you want everyone to know!

There are moments from my years of missionary work that still rise up in me when I close my eyes. They have not faded. One of them happened years ago in Nicaragua.

A friend and I had gone into a very rural community to help the poor and needy. It was a place marked by extreme poverty, dirt floors, no running water, and no nearby doctors. While we were there, a young man came toward me carrying his son in his arms. He told us the child could not urinate. There were no doctors for miles. He said the boy was dying, and he asked if I would pray.

Through my friend, who was translating, I asked the father, "Do you believe that if I pray for your son, he will be healed?" The father nodded his head "yes" with urgency. I then told my friend to tell the father that his faith was stronger than mine. I was in absolute awe of his faith. The father tenderly lifted up his young son and held him out in front of me as I got ready to pray. The Lord told me, "Greg, close your eyes."

At that time in my life, I only had one child, my son Jeremy, and he was about the same age as that little boy. After a few moments, the Lord said, "Open your eyes."

When I opened them, I saw Jeremy's head as if superimposed on that child's body. Then the Lord said, "Pray with everything you have like it's your son." I began to weep and shake. I placed my hands on that precious angel and interceded on his behalf. My soul cried out for all the pain and suffering he had endured.

The child was healed. The miracle was not because I got all the words right. The healing was the Lord's. But Jesus taught me something that day that I have carried with me ever since. He taught me to always pray like it is one of my own.

If it is a child, pray like it is your child. If it is a woman, pray like it is your wife or daughter. If it is a man, pray like it is your father, your brother, or your son. In other words, do not pray from a distance or in a mechanical sort of way. Let compassion close the gap. Let love step into the burden. Let yourself feel their pain enough to truly intercede.

What I did not realize then was that the lesson God taught me in Nicaragua would confront me years later in those hospital rooms. I had learned how to pray for others with urgency. I knew how to contend for their healing. I knew how to cry out to God for their lives as though they were my own. But when it came to my own suffering, I found myself in unfamiliar territory. I did not always know how to pray for myself even. I did not know what to do with my own weakness.

There came a point, late one night, through tears and exhaustion, that I asked God again, *Father, where are You? Why can't I feel You when I need You the most?*

Then, in one of my darkest moments, I closed my eyes and had a vision of Jesus.

With tears streaming down my face, I heard Him say, "Greg, I was there for every procedure. I was there for every scan. I was there through every long night. I was there when you could not breathe right. I was there when you were afraid. I was there when you thought you could not go on. I was there even when you could not feel Me."

Here is what I had to learn myself, and what I want you to always remember. Don't mistake God's silence for absence. The same Savior who hung on a cross, endured suffering, and overcame death is with you in the battle. He is not standing at a distance, waiting for you to pull yourself together. He is *Emmanuel,* "God with us," and He is often closest in the places where we feel Him least. Jesus never leaves us. He was there the whole time with me, and He is here with you too. Please do not ever forget that.

THE SECOND MIRACLE

There was another miracle in my life, and I would be wrong not to tell you about it.

When I left the hospital, I was on dialysis. My kidneys were failing, and once I got home, I went to treatment several times a week. That facility became a battlefield of its own. People came in on stretchers and left on stretchers. Some arrived already missing limbs. The atmosphere was dark, heavy, and hopeless. Suffering seemed to hang in the air like a stench. I tried to make the best of it. I would joke with the nurses and pretend I was there for a spa day. "Am I getting a manicure or a pedicure today?" I would tease. But those smiles only took me so far. I absolutely despised dialysis.

After everything I had already endured, I came to a point one day when something in me rose up and said, "I'm not doing this anymore. My kidneys are going to have to figure it out on their own." That may sound ridiculous, but it is the truth. I had reached my limit. And to this day, I have never received dialysis again.

Eventually, my lungs also regained strength, and that's another blessing. It's all quite extraordinary.

My greatest battle these days is learning to live in my new body. The emotional and psychological impact still lingers. Western culture likes compartments; we try to separate body from soul, emotions from spirit, as if each part can be understood on its own. But that isn't how we are made. What we walk through does not stay in one place. Trauma settles into the body, grief touches the mind, and pain moves through every layer of who we are. You cannot fully heal one part without acknowledging the others.

In Hebrew thought, the person is integrated. The heart, soul, mind, body, memory, and spirit are bound up together before God. Scripture reflects this constantly. Proverbs says, *A crushed spirit dries up the bones* (Proverbs 17:22 ESV). David laments in Psalm 31:9-10 (NIV), *Be merciful to me, Lord, for I am in distress; my eyes grow weak with sorrow, my soul and body with grief. My life is consumed by anguish and my years by groaning; my strength fails because of my affliction, and my bones grow weak.*

The word translated *body* in Hebrew points to the inner parts, the inward being, the place where emotions and pain are deeply felt. David is describing a level of distress that is not surface-level; it is reaching into every inch of who he is. This is a real human experience, written into the Word of God. As believers, and especially as leaders, we have to do a better job of talking about soul-suffering. The silence around it has cost us too much.

Complex trauma changes a person, and we should never minimize the full weight of layered grief and suffering. That is why a soldier can come home from war and wake up in a cold sweat, still on the battlefield in his mind. That is why an emergency worker can respond to thousands of calls and still have one image that never fully leaves. That is why a woman who has been violated may be completely safe and still have her body respond as though she is not. That is why a child who grew up in chaos can become a grown adult and still flinch at a raised voice. That is why a hospital patient can be years into recovery and still feel his chest tighten the moment it's time to get blood drawn.

These things are real, and Jesus understands them all. He is not put off by the psychological or emotional side of suffering. He is *a man of sorrows and acquainted with grief* (Isaiah 53:3 ESV). Throughout His earthly ministry, He healed people in ways that were often deeper and more personal than just physical restoration. He not only opened blind eyes, He also restored identity. He did not only make the lame walk, He also spoke to the places where shame and isolation had taken root. He not only cleansed lepers, He also touched the untouchable and brought them back into the community.

Again and again, Jesus shows us that healing is not confined to one dimension. He addresses the body, the mind, the soul, and the spirit together, because He sees the whole person standing before Him. If you study Jesus closely, especially in the way He healed the sick, He often gave people more than healing – He gave them a next step. He spoke words like, *"Get up, take up your bed, and walk"* (John 5:8 ESV). *"Stand up"* (Luke 17:19 NLT). *"Go in peace"* (Luke 8:48 ESV, NLT, NIV). Jesus was always propelling people forward.

Complex trauma can leave people numb, frozen, disoriented, and unsure of how to reenter life. But Jesus knows this. He is kind. He is tender. He is full of wisdom in the way He ministers to wounded people. He does not shame us for being stuck. He meets us there, and in His love, He gently speaks to us, calling us to move again.

During the last two years, I have seen so much healing, but now I am learning how to walk in the aftermath of it all. My soul is still catching up, and even that is part of the miracle.

THE LIFE I HAVE NOW

Life looks different for me now than it once did. I still have the joy of sharing the living Word with the beloved community at Beth Yeshua, and I carry a deep gratitude for them. I am also open to whatever God has for me in this next season, even when I cannot yet see what it will be.

My four children are adults now, and each of them is flourishing in his or her own way and in their own calling. I am so proud of them. Bernadette is still Bernadette. She's vivacious, strong, full of life, a remarkable wife and mother, and always serving others in one way or another. In many respects, she is still recovering from all we endured during my hospital stay and the long, unpredictable aftermath that followed. Not long ago, we went for a walk on the beach together. We were both so excited to be out there, taking it all in, but my body was not cooperating the way I had hoped. Before long, I had to call an Uber to get back. Even in that moment, she never once made me feel like a burden.

I thank God for Bernadette more than words can express. She kept fighting for me when I was too weak to fight for myself, and even now, she continues to stand beside me with grace and compassion. Before writing this book, I asked her what she remembered most from that season. Here's what she had to say:

"After the surgery to remove Greg's aorta, I believed he would recover. What I did not know was to what extent. That part was hidden. I did not know how much strength would return, how long it would take, or what life would look like on the other side. But I believed he was coming through. What mattered to me was that Greg kept fighting. I believed the Lord wanted him here, but Greg had to do the work too. He had to endure. He had to keep going. Thank God he had lived a disciplined life, because that mattered in the fight. I did not know how painful it would be. But I knew God would use it all.

"Because of Greg's health history, we are always prepared for the worst. That is just part of our reality. This time was rough, very rough, but even then, I did not believe it was his time. With God, there was always hope.

"That said, I got tired. I got tired of the daily hospital routine, the antiseptic smells, the screams of patients, the tears of visitors, and the emotional weight of walking into that place every single day. I knew Greg could not handle much more of it either. We were both worn down in different ways. But I kept going, because what else do you do when you love someone? You keep showing up. You keep praying. You keep believing. And in the end, God came through."

THE SUN ROSE UPON HIM

There is a gym on the edge of town that I drive to several times a week now. I chose it specifically because I was hoping not to run into anyone I know from the synagogue or the community. I am not hiding from people so much as I am hiding from this new version of myself. So much of my identity was wrapped up in capability, endurance, and being the man other people leaned on. That man is gone, and some mornings I grieve over him more than I expected to.

When I look in the mirror, I hardly recognize the man staring back at me. Each day, I go through what I call my old-man workout at the gym. It is humbling, even a little humiliating, but I still show up. I lace up my shoes, wobble to the car, make the drive, and do what I can, because showing up is what I have right now. I have decided that it is enough.

Not long ago, a couple from the synagogue spotted me there. I had chosen that gym specifically to avoid exactly that, and yet there they were, warm, gracious, and genuinely glad to see me. The woman asked how I was doing, and I answered honestly. "Well, I do not love the way I am living right now. It's still very hard, but I am doing my best. I do know that I cannot leave the synagogue just yet."

Then I said something that surprised even me as I heard it come out of my mouth.

"You think you need me. The truth is, I need you."

And I meant every word of it. After everything I have been through, I have come to understand how deeply we all need purpose: a reason to keep going. Without it, something in a person can begin to come undone. Routine matters. It steadies the mind when everything else feels uncertain. Without it, we slowly lose our footing. I need the rhythm of Beth Yeshua. I need the joy of teaching the gospel. I need the faces, the people, and the community of believers. So for now, I will keep serving, keep preaching, and keep pouring into the next generation of leaders until Jesus makes it clear that my assignment there is over.

I am still becoming who I am on the other side of all this. I sometimes catch myself in moments when something rises to the surface that I thought I had already dealt with. I still find that the emotional part of surviving something catastrophic does not resolve on a schedule. The body remembers. The mind keeps processing. The soul carries impressions that do not disappear just because time has passed. That is true for me, and I suspect it is true for many of you too.

When I catch my thoughts drifting into fear, sorrow, or old places of torment, I have to bring them back under the Word of God and remember Paul's instructions: *Finally, brothers, whatever is true, whatever is honorable, whatever is just, whatever is pure, whatever is lovely, whatever is commendable, if there is any excellence, if there is anything worthy of praise, think about these things* (Philippians 4:8 ESV). It's discipleship of the mind.

When Jacob wrestled with God, he wrestled at Peniel. In Hebrew, the location means "Face of God." It was there, in the dark, in the place of struggle, that he was brought to the end of himself. It was there that the schemer became the surrendered man. It was there that he was wounded, blessed, renamed, and marked. And Scripture tells us that as he crossed over and moved forward into his future, *the sun rose upon him* (Genesis 32:31 ESV). That detail means more to me now than it ever did before. The sun rose as Jacob moved forward. Not before the struggle. Not before the limp. Not before the surrender.

After.

That is how it often is with God. The light does not always break through when we think it should. But it does come. Morning does come. The sun does rise.

Now, when I wake up and see the light of another day, I tell Jesus, "Thank You. Thank You for one more morning. Thank You for one more sunrise. Thank You for one more day to love, to pray, to bless, to speak, to serve, and to simply be here." In Luke 17, Jesus healed ten lepers, but only one returned to give thanks, and he did it with a loud voice. If you take anything from me, remember this: *Be the one.* Be the one who returns. Be the one who notices the mercy of God and proclaims it for all to hear. Be the one who lifts your voice and tells your Healer, "Thank You."

Psalm 30 became very precious to me during my hospital stay. I read it often. I clung to it. It gave language to places in me that had no words of their own. *Weeping may tarry for the night, but joy comes in the morning* (Psalm 30:5 ESV). That verse is not sentimental to me. It is not decorative. It is a blood-earned truth. There were nights when weeping was all I had. There were nights when morning felt impossibly far away. But the psalm taught me to keep looking toward the light. It taught me to remember that the night does not have the final word.

My dreams and goals are different these days. They are not gone, but they have been simplified by suffering. I would love to be here to officiate one of my children's weddings. I would love, if the Lord wills, to one day hold a grandchild in my arms. Those are the kinds of desires I have now, but I also understand the reality of my situation. I understand that there are things I may never get to see on this side of Heaven. If that day never comes, then I hope maybe someday my grandchildren will read these words and know this: "You were loved before I ever held you. You were prayed for before I ever saw your face. You mattered to me because you belong to the children I love with all my heart."

I also want my children to know how proud I am of them. I want them to know how much I love them. I want them to know they do not have to perform, strive, or become something extra in order to earn that love. They are adored as they are. They do not have to carry the burden of trying to make my suffering mean something, or trying to fix what cannot be fixed. Yes, I walk slower now. I cannot go on many family vacations. Some days I am sad. Some days I am still trying to figure it out. There is no playbook for this. There is no neat guide for how to become a new man inside the shell of the old one. However, this is not their burden to carry.

Not long ago, I was with my youngest daughter Lily, and we were watching the sunset together. We sat there taking it in, the sky opening wide with color, the kind of beauty that makes you stop talking because words feel too small for what is in front of you. As we sat there, tears trickled down my cheeks. Then Lily broke the silence with a sentence that pierced me straight to the heart: "Dad, I didn't think we'd ever see another one of these together."

I knew what it had cost to sit there beside her. We both did. And I have decided that ordinary moments, when God has brought you through the fire, are not ordinary at all.

If you are reading this and you are walking through something hard right now, here is what I want you to know. God loves you so much. Your pain does not make you less visible to Him. You do not have to clean yourself up, find prettier words, or become stronger before He comes near. You do not have to earn His tenderness. You do not have to prove you are worth rescuing. Call on His name. *Jesus.* And trust that He hears you.

There will be days when your mind feels trapped in loops of fear and memory, but it does not usually mean you are failing. It means you are human, and what you went through was real. You are carrying something heavy, something that was never light to begin with, and God sees every bit of it. When the children of Israel cried out under the weight of their suffering, He did not turn away. *God heard their groaning, . . . God saw the people of Israel—and God knew* (Exodus 2:24-25 ESV). He was not distant then, and He is not distant now. He hears you. He sees you. And He is close to the brokenhearted.

If we were sitting across from each other, here is what else I would say. The same God who caused the sun to rise over Jacob can bring light to your long night. The same God who met him in the place of wrestling can meet you in the place where you feel weak, undone, and marked by all you have endured.

And I would tell you that you are absolutely cherished by our Heavenly Father. Not the future healed version of you. Not the stronger version of you. Not the version that has figured everything out and knows how to smile again without effort. You. *Right here. Right now.* In the ache. In the questions. In the trembling. In the aftermath. You are still deeply, fully, unchangingly loved.

Someday, when we are finally home with Jesus, we will

understand that our limps were never the end of the story. They were proof that the story was real. Perhaps we will sit with the saints, where there is no more pain, no more sorrow, no more crying, only the fullness of God's presence. Perhaps we will remember all that Jesus carried us through, and we will see, with clear eyes at last, that He was faithful in every moment, even the ones that felt unbearable. Perhaps we will look upon His scars, the wounds that redeemed us, and finally understand ours in a way we never could on earth.

Each morning when I lift my shirt, my eyes fall to the scar that runs down the length of my stomach. It is impossible to ignore. It catches the light in a way that reminds me it is still there, still part of me, still telling a story that my body will never forget. Yet it is a beautiful, messy reminder that I did not merely hear about God in this lifetime, I also encountered Him. I encountered His mercy. I encountered His touch and everlasting love in one of the hardest seasons of my life. The scar is not just evidence of what I went through; it is evidence of Who carried me through. And for that, I will always be grateful.

One day, every knee will bow, and every tongue will confess that Jesus the Messiah is Lord. We will see the King in His beauty. The faithful will receive the crown of life that He has promised to those who love Him. Every tear will be wiped away. Death will be no more. Mourning and pain will pass away with the former things. And there, standing in the fullness of His glory, we will finally understand that nothing we carried in this lifetime was wasted. It all brought us closer to our majestic King.

Until that day, we must fight the good fight. We must finish the race. We must keep the faith. What a glorious day it will be when our precious Savior looks us in the eyes and says, "Well done, good and faithful servant."

understand that our limps weren't the end of the story. They were proof that the story was real. Perhaps we will sit with the saints, where there is no more pain, no more sorrow, no more crying, only the fullness of God's presence. Perhaps we will remember all that Jesus carried us through and we will see with clear eyes at last that He was faithful in every moment, even the ones that felt unbearable. Perhaps we will look upon His scars, the wounds that redeemed us, and finally understand ours in a way we never could on earth.

Each morning when I lift my shirt, my eyes fall to the scar that runs down the length of my stomach. It is impossible to ignore. It catches the light in a way that reminds me it is still there, still part of me, still telling a story that my body will never forget. Yet it is a beautiful, messy reminder that I did not merely hear about God in the [illegible]. I also encountered firsthand [illegible] His [illegible]. I've [illegible] His touch and everlasting love from the hardest seasons of my life. The scar is not just evidence of what I went through; it is evidence of Who carried me through. And for that I will [illegible].

One day, every knee will bow, and every tongue will [illegible] [illegible] [illegible] the [illegible] has promised to those who [illegible] every tear will be wiped away. Death will be no more. All mourning and pain will pass away with the former [illegible] standing in the full [illegible] of His glory, we would finally understand that nothing we carried in [illegible] that [illegible] wasted. It all brought us closer to our majestic King.

Until that day, we must [illegible]. We must finish the race. We must keep the faith, with a [illegible] who [illegible] looks us in the eyes and says, "Well done, good and faithful servant."

AFTERWORD

DEAR READER,

THANK YOU SO MUCH FOR WALKING THROUGH THIS JOURNEY WITH ME. I did not want this book to end with my voice alone. In the following pages, a few of my children share their own testimonies of what they faced during my medical crisis and how God met them in the middle of it. For the sake of length and clarity, some portions of their stories have been condensed, while remaining faithful to their testimonies.

JEREMY HERSHBERG

When my father was first admitted to the hospital in Macon for a staph infection, the situation seemed serious, but he had overcome crises like this before, so I remained confident he would pull through. Then, around Thanksgiving, everything took a devastating turn. I followed the ambulance the entire distance as he was transferred to a hospital in Atlanta, hoping better resources would make the difference. For a moment, there was hope, but it didn't last. As tests were run and days passed, the reality became clear: my father was in grave danger.

The emergency surgery to remove his aorta happened suddenly.

There was no time to prepare, and I couldn't get there before he was taken into the operating room. The comfort I wanted to give him was reduced to a short phone call, one that felt like a final goodbye. For over thirteen hours, I waited in fear. By a miracle, he made it through. In that moment, I wasn't thinking about how far he had to go; I was just grateful he was alive.

Throughout the entire ordeal, I tried to be a source of strength for my family. I couldn't control anyone else's faith, but I knew I had to believe. There was no other outcome I was willing to accept besides my father walking out of that hospital alive. I prayed constantly. I can't say I heard a specific word from God that gave me peace, but I remained steadfast because I knew there was only One who could fix something of this magnitude.

The first time I truly thought he might not survive was when he went into surgery, nearly a thousand miles away, and I had to hear his goodbye over the phone. The second time was when he was rushed back to the hospital. I found him in the kitchen, in severe pain and coughing up blood. I drove him to the ER, and what should have been a ten-minute drive felt endless as I watched him struggle to breathe, unable to do anything but get him there.

When we arrived, I carried him inside. When I was told to stop for paperwork, I ignored it and brought him straight into the emergency room. By the grace of God, the doctor on call was a friend of his, and within seconds, he was being treated. Still, I didn't know if he would survive the hour. Thankfully, he made an incredible recovery. My faith was tested in ways I can't fully explain, but I couldn't imagine a world without my father. I held on to faith, I held on to hope, and in the end, there is no question that God performed a miracle.

MAX HERSHBERG

From the beginning, when a loved one gets sick, you kind of assume the medicine will work and the doctors will get them back to a healthy state. However, it's a different story when you start hearing, "I'm so sorry," or, "We did what we could." Reaching that point, saying you're a believer is one thing, but it becomes much heavier when God is all you have to put your faith in, whether you like it or not.

There were plenty of ups and downs over the fifty-plus days he was in the hospital and ICU, and we received a lot of bad news during that time. To me, my dad was always the biggest and the strongest, and the name Greg Hershberg was almost always met with respect – and often a little bit of fear. So to see him go from being this unstoppable guy to having the inability to even breathe was incredibly difficult. Being able to witness this entire process was painful, but God did what He does. He pulled light from darkness and gave the world yet another reason to believe.

I've always looked at my dad as someone who is indestructible, like he would bounce back from anything. But after his major surgery in Atlanta, everything changed. I waited with my mom and Lily for hours as the surgery went on, and with each update, the complications seemed to grow. By the time it was finally over, he was on life support.

I went back to see him, but I couldn't bring myself to walk into his room. I was just crying, unable to even approach him. Seeing him like that, essentially lifeless, something broke in me. For the first time, I realized I might have to go through life without my dad, and the emptiness that came with that is still hard to describe.

Later, after he was taken off life support and still couldn't speak or write, I remember thinking that I might never see the Greg Hershberg we all once knew.

In terms of frustration, it wasn't really a lack of faith, but more of a frustration with the entire situation. At the same time, I was motivated and amazed by the faith of loved ones and those who cared deeply for my dad. To be completely honest, I always felt like God would save him. Maybe that was me being foolish or naïve, but I just felt like my dad hadn't completed his mission for the Kingdom yet.

LILY HERSHBERG

My dad's health had been a challenge for most of my life, but I never believed there was anything he couldn't overcome, until I got a call late one night while I was away at college. Being hundreds of miles from home, I didn't fully understand how serious things were, but hearing his voice tremble as he told me "goodbye" before surgery made it real. I remember breaking down, stunned by how quickly everything had changed while I was so far away.

I was already trying to manage the pressure of school and being in a new environment, and suddenly I felt helpless and consumed by fear, unable to imagine life without my dad, the person who had always been my protector and source of strength. During those weeks, I tried to stay composed when around my friends, but most of the time I was pretending everything was okay while I was falling apart on the inside.

When I was finally able to return home, I could barely recognize him. The man who had always seemed so strong was now lying fragile in a hospital bed, connected to machines that were keeping him alive. Beyond that, his spirit was broken. My dad, who was always laughing and joking, was now quiet, withdrawn, and struggling.

I spent Thanksgiving in the hospital that year, realizing his recovery was only just beginning. After months of uncertainty and prayer, he was finally able to come home, but even then, it wasn't over. Not long after, he was rushed back to the hospital and placed on life support again. Experiencing that kind of hope and relief, only to have it taken away so suddenly, was overwhelming. I felt scared and confused, questioning why it was happening, but still choosing to trust that God had a plan, even when I couldn't see it.

My family and I turned to God when nothing else made sense, and I truly believe His presence carried us through. Watching my dad slowly recover, seeing him open his eyes again, speak again, and eventually take his first steps, felt like witnessing a miracle. That experience taught me not to take a single day for granted, and to cherish every moment with the people I love.

About the Author

GREG HERSHBERG was born in New York City and raised in Orthodox Judaism. He graduated from Pace University, *magna cum laude,* and later owned and operated an executive recruiting firm in New York City, specializing in banking and finance. In 1989, he married Bernadette, and while on his honeymoon in Israel, he had a visitation from the Lord that turned his heart to serving God.

In 1992, Greg became involved in the Messianic Jewish Movement and was ordained through the International Association of Messianic Congregations and Synagogues (IAMCS). He became the leader of Beth Judah Messianic Congregation. In 2002, the Lord moved Greg and his family to Macon, Georgia, to lead Congregation Beth Yeshua.

The ministry went global in 2010, and Congregation Beth Yeshua became Beth Yeshua International (BYI). What was a local storefront congregation became an international ministry and training center in Macon, Georgia, with congregations and schools in India, Kenya, Australia, Germany, Israel, and across America. In addition, Greg's messages are live-streamed throughout the world. More about Greg can be found in his autobiography, *From the Projects to the Palace: A Rags to Riches to True Riches Story.*

www.bethyeshuainternational.org

BOOKS ALSO BY THE AUTHOR

Things God Hates, Things God Loves

Scripture says that the Lord will *look with favor* on the one who is humble and contrite and who trembles at His Word. This word *look* in Hebrew is nabat, and it means "to regard, to consider, or to pay attention to." In plain words, we're told that the God-fearing person who *hates what He hates and loves what He loves* is the one the Lord pays favorable attention to.

To experience the favor of God is amazing and incredible, to say the least. Journey through this book with me and consider the Scriptures that tell us what the Lord hates and what He loves. Ask the Lord to teach you to live with all your heart, soul, mind, and strength for Him, in such a way that He will look upon you with favor.

Available where books are sold.

A Life for God

To grasp the depth and height of the great I AM and to live life with the end (eternity) in sight is a believer's most significant accomplishment. Within each of His chosen people, God has placed a desire to know Him, to worship Him, and to live victoriously for Him. He has shown us how to have the right perspective concerning this life and the one to come. And what God starts, He finishes.

Come, let Messianic Rabbi Greg Hershberg open the Torah and give you glimpses of the incredible love and character of our God. Let him point you to the Savior through the offerings of Leviticus and the mournful lament of Psalm 22. Let him guide you through the greatest commandment as you learn to say "no" to yourself, pick up your execution-stake, and follow the great I AM.

Available where books are sold.

Don't Die in Your Sins

People are obsessed with life; no one wants to die. In fact, we are scared to death of dying.

For most people, death is either a great mystery or a subject of great denial. However, the fact remains – we all die. What if this life is not all there is? What if there actually is life after death? If so, who can tell us what happens after we die? Because of His firsthand experience in heaven and His knowledge of the future, Jesus can. He presents us with three basic truths about the subject of life after death:

1. There is life after death.
2. There are two destinations from which everyone must choose.
3. There is a way to ensure you make the right choice.

Right now, you may be dying of thirst, but you don't have to perish in your thirst. Likewise, you may be overcome with sin, but you don't have to die in your sins. There is something you can do, right now, to ensure that when you die, you will have everlasting life and happiness.

Available where books are sold.

www.ingramcontent.com/pod-product-compliance
Lightning Source LLC
LaVergne TN
LVHW010606160826
845677LV00013B/3281

* 9 7 9 8 8 8 9 3 6 5 8 6 0 *